CW00678215

PREACHING BY HEART

PREACHING *by* HEART

How a classical practice
helps contemporary pastors to preach without notes

⇓

Ryan P. Tinetti

FOREWORD BY *Richard Lischer*

CASCADE *Books* · Eugene, Oregon

PREACHING BY HEART
How a Classical Practice Helps Contemporary Pastors to Preach without Notes

Copyright © 2021 Ryan Tinetti. All rights reserved. Except for brief
quotations in critical publications or reviews, no part of this book may
be reproduced in any manner without prior written permission from the
publisher. Write: Permissions, Wipf and Stock Publishers, 199 W. 8th Ave.,
Suite 3, Eugene, OR 97401.

Cascade Books
An Imprint of Wipf and Stock Publishers
199 W. 8th Ave., Suite 3
Eugene, OR 97401

www.wipfandstock.com

PAPERBACK ISBN: 978-1-7252-6951-4
HARDCOVER ISBN: 978-1-7252-6950-7
EBOOK ISBN: 978-1-7252-6952-1

Cataloguing-in-Publication data:

Names: Tinetti, Ryan, author. | Richard Lischer, foreword.

Title: Preaching by heart : how a classical practice helps contemporary pastors to preach without notes / Ryan Tinetti with a foreword by Richard
Lischer.

Description: Eugene, OR: Cascade Books, 2021 | Includes bibliographical
references.

Identifiers: ISBN 978-1-7252-6951-4 (paperback) | ISBN 978-1-7252-6950-7
(hardcover) | ISBN 978-1-7252-6952-1 (ebook)

Subjects: LCSH: Extemporaneous preaching. | Preaching—History—Early
church, ca. 30–600.

Classification: BV4235.E8 T3 2021 (print) | BV4235 (ebook)

To Anne,
who knows me by heart

Table of Contents

Foreword

I BELIEVE THERE IS a secret passage that extends from the brain by way of the heart to the tongue. Preachers are always looking for it in hopes that the sermon they have conceived will be more natural or believable when it is delivered. The problems they/we face in making this journey are numerous: there is the time-gap that inevitably exists between the point of conception and the moment of delivery. This led Dietrich Bonhoeffer to claim that the sermon must be "twice born," once in the study and once in the pulpit. One the other hand, if there is no gap between conception and delivery (note the metaphors), it means the preacher is speaking extemporaneously or off the cuff, which sometimes works in urgent situations but as a homiletical practice is disastrous.

A second difficulty has to do with the method by which we create our sermons: We write them. Before we preach them orally to an empty chancel, to ourselves, or to the dog, we tap them out on a laptop. We move from text to text rather than text to tongue. The written manuscript then becomes an entity an end in itself, to which its author becomes so devoted that he or she will strive to preach only what is written, producing in the preacher an awkward concentration on the manuscript rather than attention to the congregation. This leads to a fork in the homiletical road: one way leads to the practice of reading the manuscript, with appropriate intonation and feeling, of course. The other leads to the mind-numbing task of memorizing the manuscript word for word, and to do so week in and week out.

A further problem has to do with the audience. Most audiences do not respond interactively and receptively to either a read sermon or a carefully memorized manuscript. The novelist E. M. Forester said of writing, "Only connect." Neither reading nor memorizing readily connects with hearers who crave the natural rhythms of authentic speech. The readers and memorizers of sermons often blame today's communications atmosphere, or sensorium, which includes teleprompters and flawlessly fluid media personalities, for creating impossibly high standards of communication. But in truth, ancient audiences were as unreceptive to the reading of speeches as we are.

Preaching by Heart restores memory to its important position in the office of preaching. To the ancients, memory was an indispensable element in the delivery of speeches, and the great speakers were their culture's foremost trainers of memory. The preacher Augustine was both the rhetorical and theological master of what has become a forgotten subject among preachers. His reflections on memory in the *Confessions* also enriched his homiletics. Print culture reduced the role of memory in most fields of endeavor; technology has obliterated it. Whatever it is we fail to locate in what Augustine called "the mansions of memory" can be found on YouTube. Today's helps and devices—"extra-mental storage arrangements" in Walter Ong's phrase—seem to have erased memory from the preacher's to-do list.

The Christian congregation—as opposed to an "audience"—has a deeper, more theological measuring stick for sermon delivery. The nature of the gospel argues against artifice.

Jesus wrote nothing, but he spoke with authority and not as the religious professionals of his day. When he spoke everyone listened, and all who heard were either healed or cut to the quick, sometimes both. Although Paul insists, "We do not proclaim ourselves, but Jesus Christ as Lord . . . ," everyone understands that God's word passes through the intellect, heart, passions, and lips of the preacher. The ultimate authenticity of the sermon rests on its coherence with the scriptural text; its secondary authenticity, if we may call it that, emerges from the manner in which it is delivered—and lived—by the speaker.

Preaching by Heart charts a way through the impasse of sermon delivery. It offers a method that involves both mind and heart in a realistic way. Ryan Tinetti explores the ancient tradition of the memory palace, an old and reliable practice of associating the key elements of the sermon with visual markers, with the result that the preacher does not so much render a manuscript as *move* through a message with the help of easily recognized guideposts. By analogy, one thinks of story-boarding a sermon or blocking a stage performance.

As a teacher I sometimes compared sermon delivery to crossing a creek by means of several well-delineated stepping stones. Memory plus movement is everything. What Tinetti presents in this book is a method far more specific and sophisticated, yet extremely simple to implement. It will also enable preachers to evaluate their sermons and to chart and clarify the paths they have taken from idea to delivery. With the centrality of memory reestablished, preachers will be challenged to *use* (as in exercise) their memory.

Tinetti skillfully shows how memory works not only in the delivery but also in the creation of the sermon. In a visual culture like ours his stress on the *oral* nature of sermon preparation is an overdue corrective to literary assessments of the sermon. *Preaching by Heart* will empower preachers to remember what they wish to say without denaturing its impact by reading or word-for-word memorization.

And best of all, it offers a passage from brain to tongue that does not bypass the heart.

Richard Lischer
Durham, NC

INTRODUCTION

Preaching By Heart

The challenge of memory in preaching

"I WILL COMBINE MEMORY and delivery in one of the few sweeping generalizations I can make about preaching through the ages," writes O. C. Edwards, Jr., in his exhaustive *History of Preaching*. "Which is that, with rare exceptions, the most effective preachers have not preached from manuscripts."[1] Pastors know this all too well. They devote a week or more to thoughtful, Spirit-filled preparation to preach: studying the Scriptures, reading commentaries, wrestling to discern the text's present significance as well as its original meaning, and of course praying. The culmination of this preparation is that, Lord willing, they not only *have to say* something; they *have something to say*. They have a word from the Lord to his gathered people; a message from the heart. As St. Paul told the Corinthians: "We have spoken freely to you, Corinthians; our heart is wide open" (2 Cor 6:11). But indeed this message comes not merely from their own all-too-human hearts, but from

---

1. Edwards Jr., *A History of Preaching*, 836. Edwards goes on to make a statement that anticipates the thesis of the present book: "In not doing so they have to an extent honored the standard of the Greco-Roman rhetoricians, who either memorized their orations or spoke them extemporaneously."

1

the very heart of God. Its glad and believing reception is therefore of the utmost importance.

But here is where the challenge presents itself. The preacher steps up to the pulpit with the word of God for the people of God. The congregation looks on in expectation. The preacher returns their gaze, poised and prepared, and then . . . looks down *to read.* Enthusiastically, perhaps, even dramatically (like Orson Welles in a radio theater), but read nevertheless.[2] And just like that, the intimate connection between preacher and people, between God's heart and the heart of the church, is interrupted by an interloper: the preacher's notes. The link has not been severed, to be sure; the word can still work. And yet there may be a discomfiting sense— for the preacher, if not also for the people—that some degree of connection has been lost.

The difficulty is long-standing. "Memory, or the lack of it," writes Clyde Fant, "presents a unique and often frustrating challenge to preachers." He goes on to delineate this challenge's many facets:

> Should the problems of remembering the sermon be eliminated by the writing and reading of a manuscript? Or should notes alone, whether extensive or meager, be taken into the pulpit and memory be trusted for the balance? Or should written materials be avoided altogether in delivering the sermon? And if so, should the sermon be memorized line by line from a previously written manuscript? What place, if any, should memory play in the delivery of a sermon?[3]

Fant has outlined several approaches to the challenge of memory in preaching. The first and arguably most common approach is to preach *from the page.* Thus the preacher will write out a complete manuscript and take it to the pulpit or platform, or else

---

2. As John Broadus remarked in 1870, preachers who read their sermons "scarcely ever raise us higher than to feel that really this man reads almost like speaking" (Broadus, *A Treatise on the Preparation and Delivery of Sermons,* 444).

3. Fant, "Memory," 331–32.

devise an outline from which to speak. In this case, the concern for memory has been addressed by largely removing the need for its use, as Plato famously argued, by means of the written word.[4] This has the benefit of giving the preachers the confidence of knowing just what they will say, which is no small thing. Its drawback, though, as has already been alluded to, is that it disrupts the connection between pastor and people. But more than that, as we will see presently, preaching from the page can also compromise the preacher's credibility.

The second approach, which swings in the complete opposite direction, is to preach, so to speak, *from the hip*. Sometimes known as "impromptu preaching," to preach from the hip is to supplant memory with (supposedly Spirit-driven) spontaneity. In this regard Jesus' words in Matthew are appealed to: "When they deliver you over, do not be anxious how you are to speak or what you are to say, for what you are to say will be given to you in that hour. For it is not you who speak, but the Spirit of your Father speaking through you" (Matt 10:19–20). Hugh Oliphant Old observes that "many preachers have used this as a justification for impromptu preaching on all occasions."[5] Traditionally associated with the Quakers, Pentecostals, and some African American preaching, in its more extreme forms impromptu preaching may purposefully eschew preparation lest the Holy Spirit's pathway be hindered by the preacher's own pondering.[6] In endeavoring to be free of memory, however, this method threatens to become free of meaning.[7]

4. See his critique in *Phaedrus*, in which he has a King Thamus saying (through Socrates): "If men learn this [writing], it will implant forgetfulness in their souls; they will cease to exercise memory because they rely on that which is written, calling things to remembrance no longer from within themselves, but by means of external marks" (§274c–275 b).

5. Old, *The Reading and Preaching of the Scriptures in the Worship of the Christian Church*, 142.

6. See Graves, "Ministry and Preaching," in *The Oxford Handbook of Quaker Studies*, chapter 18.

7. Pattison, in *The Making of the Sermon*, criticizes the impromptu approach with the following anecdote: "'My Lord,' a clergyman once boasted to his bishop, 'when I go up the steps of the pulpit I never know the subject of my sermon'; and the bishop answered him, 'No, and I hear that your congregation

The third approach is in one sense a moderating position and in another its own extreme—what we might call preaching *from the head*. This is the sort of preaching in which, as Fant puts it, the sermon is "memorized line by line from a previously written manuscript." While this might seem at first to resolve the challenge of memory, upon further examination it merely magnifies it. Now the preacher is tightrope walking in the pulpit, attempting to remember lines like a Broadway actor. Even where this approach is done successfully, however—which is to say, where the preacher manages not to forget the text of the sermon—it easily lapses into what my friend Richard Lischer refers to as "reading the teleprompter in your head."

Preaching from the page, from the hip, and from the head: each of these approaches in their own way addresses the problem of memory. And while they each have their positive attributes, they also have significant flaws. Another alternative is needed.

Preaching by heart

I would like to suggest that a more salutary approach is preaching *by heart*.[8] In one respect, this approach is a combination of the best features of each of the other three mentioned: the preparation that comes with preaching from the page, the Spirit-led spontaneity of preaching from the hip, and the commitment to memory of preaching from the head. In another respect, however, preaching by heart is more than a mere patchwork quilt of other ideas; it is, rather, its own distinct approach to sermon delivery and even, as we shall see, to sermon preparation.

---

does not when you come down'" (322).

8. What I have called "preaching by heart" most clearly has resonances with what has sometimes been known as "extemporaneous preaching," though this term is rather facile and given to abuse (for instance, it can be used synonymously with impromptu preaching). See Ware Jr., *Hints on Extemporaneous Preaching*. Cf. also Quintilian, *Institutio Oratoria* 10.7: "The greatest fruit of our studies, the richest harvest of our long labors, is *the ability to speak extemporaneously*" (*ex tempore dicendi facultas*).

What, then, do I mean by "preaching by heart"? The concept comprises several elements. Haddon Robinson, echoing concerns already raised, elucidates the first:

> Your sermon should not be read to a congregation. Reading usually kills a lively sense of communication. Neither should you try to memorize your manuscript. Not only does memorization place a hefty burden on you if you speak several times a week, but an audience senses when you are reading words of the wall of your mind. Agonize with thought and words at your desk, and what you write will be internalized.[9]

The sermon being *internalized* is a helpful concept and the essential element of preaching by heart.[10] One calls to mind the traditional Collect for the Word, in which we aspire to "hear, read, mark, learn, and *inwardly digest*" the Holy Scriptures. So preachers also aspire to "inwardly digest" the message of the sermon so that it, in a sense, becomes part of them. Thomas Long, furthering the thought, advises preachers to practice their sermon such that they "absorb it": "We do not memorize it, but we learn it 'by heart' and, thus, can be more present with and for the hearers in the actual event of preaching."[11]

A second element to preaching by heart is the one that has been most commonly associated with this conversation in recent years—namely, that the proclamation occurs *without notes*.[12] The notion of "preaching without notes," about which more below, has

---

9. Robinson, *Biblical Preaching*, 185–86.

10. For some readers this may raise the question of what form the sermon should initially be composed in: manuscript, outline, etc. For present purposes, however, I will remain indifferent to the question, though in chapter 3 I will make my own recommendation that I call "sketching the sermon." Whether the preacher writes out all of the sermon or none of the sermon beforehand is immaterial at this point. All that is presupposed is a prepared message, whatever form it may take.

11. Long, *The Witness of Preaching*, 269.

12. The phrase was evidently popularized by Charles Koller in his book *How to Preach without Notes*, originally published as *Expository Preaching without Notes*.

much in common our concept of "preaching by heart." The principal contrast I wish to draw is that the former has the potential for confusing the means and the end. Our goal is not to be *sans* notes, *per se*; that is more of a by-product or necessary precondition for something more. That "something more" is the third element of preaching by heart.

In the *Rhetorica ad Herennium*, a rhetorical treatise from the first century before Christ, the unknown author[13] wrote, "This one must remember: good delivery ensures that what the orator is saying *seems to come from his heart*."[14] Why this is so significant for preachers we will return to presently, but suffice it to say at the moment that if such authenticity mattered for classical orators, many of whom were peddling messages merely for profit or acclaim (as with the Sophists), then it should matter all the more for Christian heralds of the free grace of Christ in the gospel.

Now we have all the elements in place in order to offer a technical definition of our concept of preaching by heart. It is neither mere memorization nor impromptu *ex corde* utterance. Rather, *preaching by heart is proclamation in which the essential message of the sermon becomes so internalized by the preacher that he or she can stand before the people of God and proclaim it without notes as an authentically Spirit-prompted utterance.* In other words, preaching by heart is proclamation in which there is harmony between preachers' message and their manner, between their heart and their delivery.

The linguistic phrase "preaching by heart" evokes two other significant features. First, the phrase "learn by heart" is a common idiom to describe committing something to memory.[15] For the

---

13. In the introduction to his translation of the work for the Loeb Classical Library, Harry Caplan writes, "Although the belief in Ciceronian authorship has still not entirely disappeared, all the recent editors agree that the attribution is erroneous" (Pseudo-Cicero, *Rhetorica ad Herennium*, ix). Throughout this book we will follow the Loeb's lead and refer to the author as Pseudo-Cicero.

14. *Ex animo agi videatur.* Pseudo-Cicero, *Rhetorica ad Herennium* III.27.

15. "Preach (or learn) by heart" is also more apt than the simple notion of "memorization," since it avoids the negative connotations that, as we have observed above, can come with that latter word.

Christian "learning by heart" might even call to mind the Psalm: "I have hidden your word in my heart that I might not sin against you" (119:11 NIV). To learn something by heart suggests not merely that you have hammered it into your head, but that you have, as we say, "taken it to heart."

Secondly, and following from this, preaching "by heart" bears resemblance (without being identical) to the notion of something coming "from the heart." This phrase is not unproblematic. It can suggest a soppy sentimentalism or anti-intellectual emotionalism; that is not the intention here. Rather, it is echoed in order to capture the sense that the preacher is himself implicated in the message and invested in it. While it is certainly true that St. Paul could rejoice that "in every way, whether in pretense or in truth, Christ is proclaimed" (Phil 1:18), all things being equal the church rightly desires preachers who are personally committed to their message.

Why preaching by heart matters

Before moving forward, we should comment upon an assumption of the present author and an animating purpose for this book, which has been hinted at in the foregoing discussion. The assumption, simply put, is that *preachers actually believe what they preach.* Sophists and false prophets can *seem* genuine without actually being so. The problem that stems from the challenge of memory for many faithful preachers is the reverse: they can *be* genuine without *seeming* so. A disconnect can thus arise between preachers' reality and their perception by the congregation. Their delivery belies their beliefs. And this brings us face to face with the issue of why preaching by heart is so vitally important.

Perhaps we can get at this by way of an illustration from the popular Netflix drama *The Crown*, which traces the life and reign of Queen Elizabeth II. One episode recounts the growing public dissent and even derision that the queen was receiving in the late 1950s. Much of this stemmed from her public speaking skills, or lack thereof. The matter comes to a head when a small-time journalist known as Lord Altrincham pens an op-ed criticizing the Queen's practice of reading her addresses from a manuscript. A mix of both public agreement and opprobrium ensues, and so Lord Altrincham is invited to defend his remarks on a television news program. The host presses him: "Judging from your article, you'd like the Queen to have the qualities of a wit, you'd like her to be a better orator, a TV personality, in addition to being a diligent, dutiful, and devoted monarch and a mother."[16] But the journalist responds in a way that may speak to preachers as well: "All I'm suggesting is that, in her public speeches and in her appearances, she should be more, uh, *natural*. Her style of speaking is, quite frankly, a pain in the neck. She sounds strangled. I had the misfortune of hearing one of the Queen's speeches in a dental waiting room recently. I was horrified by the indifference and inertia with which the speech was greeted."

What Lord Altrincham is insisting, and what the Queen herself grudgingly comes to accept, is that her inability to speak without notes was ultimately a crisis of credibility.[17] If she herself was not sufficiently convinced and gripped by her message so as to deliver it "by heart," so to speak, how could—or should—her people be? And if that was true for the Crown of England, how much more so for us who claim to speak on behalf of the Crown of all creation?

In his book *Communicating for a Change*, Andy Stanley drills down on this theme of credibility.[18] He makes the analogy to an actor, that no performer worth his weight in salt would walk on stage with script in hand. "Like a good actor," he writes, "you've got to be believable":

16. Pastors may have flashbacks here: "In addition to being a devoted shepherd, I must be a better orator, a TV personality, a CEO, marketing expert . . ."

17. In the terms of classical rhetoric, this is an *ethos* problem. We will explore this further in the next chapter.

18. According to the "modes of persuasion" in classical rhetoric, this would be *ethos*: the personal character of the speaker. Here the focus is narrowly on memorization in preaching, but of course *ethos* comprises numerous aspects concerning the character and authority of the speaker. See Aristotle, *Ars Rhetorica* II.1368a.

After all, you actually believe! People are expecting you to engage them on multiple levels. And in light of what's at stake, you should be both engaging and convincing. If an actor is willing to memorize and internalize a script in order to convince you that he or she is someone other than who they really are, how motivated should we be to internalize our messages in order to convince our audience that we really are who we claim to be?[19]

At its root, then, the inability to preach by heart presents a *pastoral* problem: preachers are not able to have the same degree of personal connectedness with their congregations, their credibility is compromised, and so the effectiveness of the proclamation suffers.[20]

We might also note in passing that failure to preach by heart also presents (in a variety of forms) a *practical* problem: needing some manner of notes, whether that be a full manuscript or even just an outline, keeps the preacher tied to the pulpit or lectern like an astronaut tethered to her shuttle.[21] Neither wants to be lost in space, but as a result the amount of exploration is limited.

Practical challenges aside, however, it is the threat to credibility that makes preaching by heart such a pressing concern for pastors. For Christians (preachers included!), the power of persuasion—indeed, conversion—rests with the word of God. But if that word is not heard on account of the proclaimer's oratory, if the message is undermined by the messenger, then the Spirit's work is stunted. To be sure, as Luther would remind us, the God who could speak through a donkey can speak through inadequate preachers no less. But most preachers would agree that this is not an excuse for giving anything less than their best. We are ambassadors for the King; how could we but own His good news for ourselves? Stanley writes, "I find something very disingenuous about

19. Stanley, *Communicating for a Change*, 133–34.

20. On a personal level, feelings of inadequacy and uncertainty may also arise in the heart of the preacher.

21. One colleague tells me that she learned to preach from memory during a summer serving at a Christian camp whose outdoor chapel lacked a pulpit or any kind of lectern. "Necessity," etc.

the speaker who says, 'This is very, very important,' and then reads something from his notes . . . Every effective communicator must figure out how to internalize all of and memorize a majority of his or her message."[22] So the question is: how?[23]

"Preaching without notes": other solutions

Homiletics textbooks routinely address the task of memorization and delivery, but even the best ones tend not to offer substantive practical guidance in accomplishing it.[24] For example, Donald Sunukjian, after discouraging the use of notes by preachers, quickly qualifies, "I'm not suggesting that you memorize your message. But I am suggesting that if you have a clear outline, have worked on your wording, and have gone over the message several times . . . then you *will* be able to deliver it freely without notes."[25] This may be true, but the counsel undoubtedly leaves something to be desired since it lacks a plain path to accomplishing the goal.

In addition to the textbook treatments of preparation for sermon delivery, there are a pair of monographs that have gone

22. Stanley, *Communicating*, 135.

23. A theological objection may be raised that, incidentally, resonates deeply with me as a Lutheran committed to the efficacy of God's word. Some could say, "The word of God never returns void, and the Bible does not add any caveats about whether or not it is read." This is a fair point and not to be denied. That said, it is surely also the case that message and messenger converge in the preaching task, and that so-called "First Article gifts"—including rhetoric—should not be eschewed. At the end of the (Sun)day, though, every preacher commits their work to God and says, with St. Paul, "I planted, Apollos watered, but God gave the growth" (1 Cor 3:6). To provide a full theological justification for the issues under consideration in this study goes beyond our scope. Suffice it to say that, in the mystery of conversion, what matters is both the power of the word and, at least to some extent, the persuasiveness of the preacher. See, e.g., the parable of the Sower (Luke 8:4–15 and parallels), in which the efficacy of the seed, the word, is dependent upon it being understood.

24. See, for example, Long, *The Witness of Preaching*, chapter 10; Robinson, *Biblical Preaching*, chapter 10; Donald Sunukjian, *Invitation to Biblical Preaching*; Paul Scott Wilson, *The Practice of Preaching*, chapter 10.

25. Sunukjian, *Invitation to Biblical Preaching*, 302.

further in providing practical directives for what we have called "preaching by heart," and that have exercised especial influence on pastors hoping to break the grip of the manuscript: Charles Koller's *How to Preach without Notes*[26] and, more recently, Joseph Webb's *Preaching without Notes*.[27] A brief review of these influential books is in order.

How to Preach without Notes

Koller catalogs the various and sundry strategies that preachers will use in order to achieve what he calls "note-free delivery."[28] While his book is now a half-century old, it is safe to say that these are still the strategies used by most pastors. First, there is the attempt to compose a manuscript and then memorize it—what we have called above "preaching from the head." Apart from the sheer practical challenge of accomplishing this feat on a weekly basis (if not more often), Koller notes that there's the danger of this coming off as more *declamation* than *proclamation*—like rhetorical push-ups instead of evangelical preaching.

Secondly, there is the practice of taking a manuscript into the pulpit but with a careful taxonomy of underlining, highlighting, or otherwise noting key statements in the sermon. Koller suggests that this method often sounds something like the oral recitation of an article abstract. The upshot is that the sermon ends up as the worst of both worlds—being neither a memorized manuscript nor an impromptu utterance, it comes off as a dance routine that only kicks in with every third or fourth step.

Finally, and what Koller himself advocates for, is the development of a "carefully prepared outline." As Koller states, "The better the outline, the greater the likelihood of its not being needed in the pulpit."[29] He then goes on to lay out a dizzyingly detailed

26. Koller, *How to Preach without Notes*. Originally published as *Expository Preaching without Notes*.

27. Webb, *Preaching without Notes*.

28. Koller, *How to Preach*, chapter 13.

29. Koller, *How to Preach* , 92.

system of points and sub-points, headings and indentations. It's an impressive device, and surely it has aided many preachers over the last half-century. One is nevertheless left with the impression that its complexity detracts from its usefulness—and in any event, it has not gone much further actually to assist the pastor to preach by heart.

Preaching without Notes

In his 2001 book *Preaching without Notes*, Joseph Webb builds on Koller's work and takes it a good bit further. To begin with, Webb situates note-free preaching within the larger context of sermon preparation: "The decision to preach a sermon without notes should be made before the sermon is prepared, not after. This is because preaching without notes requires one to prepare in some strikingly different ways than if one plans to write out and preach from a manuscript, or even to preach from an extensively worked outline."[30] Preaching without notes is thus not a stand-alone accomplishment, but the product of a broader process that begins with careful study and, indeed, diligent note-taking.

Like Koller, he advocates developing an outline to be learned by heart; unlike Koller, he focuses on what he calls "sequences" rather than a succession of points and sub-points. He writes, "This is one of the major differences between outlining the inductive sermon to be preached without notes and the older forms of sermon outlining, particularly the outlining of the deductive sermon."[31] Webb prescribes a four-step process for developing the sequences: isolating, arranging, marking, and evaluating. Such organizing is far more important to preaching without notes than mnemonic tricks: "Of all the things that recent research has taught us about the enhancement of human memory, none is more important than

---

30. Webb, *Preaching without Notes*, 35.

31. Webb, *Preaching without Notes*, 58–59.

the clear, concise organization of the materials to be memorized."[32] Well-arranged sermons run laps around acrostics any day.

He then turns to the memorization of the sermon proper—and here is where Webb's approach may leave the preacher wanting more. Helpfully, Webb suggests several factors that contribute to a strong short-term memory (physical and mental health, concentration, interest in the material, etc.).[33] Ultimately, though, he lands on the essential role of *repetition*: "There is no substitute for it . . . Only the repetition of the materials to be memorized, within the context of those factors, actually results in activating short-term memory."[34] Webb advises devoting two blocks of time to "concentrated memorization" (each about an hour long), taking a refresher hour a day later, and then giving a brief review Sunday morning. He writes, "I go through the sequence titles in order, repetitiously speaking them aloud, continuing down the list. I do it over and over again until I can almost do it without thinking about them."[35] Thus, for Webb, repetition is the key.

This is helpful counsel so far as it goes. *Repetitio mater studiorum est*, as the old maxim has it ("repetition is the mother of learning"), and in general one ought to subscribe to it wholeheartedly. But is there no better alternative to what, as Webb concedes, amounts to nose-to-the-grindstone rote learning? A recent *New York Times* article lamented,

> We think memorizing is laborious, boring work because we've been taught to do it by rote. You may recall, as I do, countless hours in third grade poring over multiplication tables or, in ninth grade, endlessly conjugating French (or Spanish) verbs, or in 11th grade, incessantly reciting Macbeth's "Tomorrow, and tomorrow, and tomorrow" soliloquy in the attempt to firmly place them

32. Webb, *Preaching without Notes*, 82–83.

33. Cf. the practical advice of Quintilian: "Learning by heart and writing have in common that both are greatly assisted by good health, good digestion, and a mind free of other distractions" (*Institutio Oratoria* 11.2 §35).

34. Quintilian, *Institutio Oratoria*, 84.

35. Quintilian, *Institutio Oratoria*, 94.

in long-term memory. These brute-force approaches are dull because they're devoid of any creativity.[36]

In modern parlance, are there no "memory hacks"? Surveying the solutions proposed by Koller, Webb, and others would apparently confirm the conclusion of Clyde Fant: "There seems to be no great secret to the art of those who preach largely from memory, no clever devices to aid in memorizing the sermon."[37]

And yet, remarkably, there remains a near-complete neglect of the method for learning by heart that enabled classical orators, Patristic preachers, and medieval missionaries to speak with confidence and persuasiveness without the benefit of any notes.[38] It is a method that "Roman senators had used to memorize their speeches, that the Athenian statesman Themistocles had supposedly used to memorize the names of twenty thousand Athenians, and that medieval scholars had used to memorize entire books."[39] It is known as the method of loci or, more affectionately, the Memory Palace.[40]

The Memory Palace (aka the Method of Loci)

In book X of his *Confessions*, St. Augustine makes a move that is not uncommon for him, particularly in that work: he starts exploring his memory. For many of us, such exploration is akin to sifting through grandma's attic. The space is cluttered with all sorts of stuff—some interesting, some not, and much of it with unclear

36. Frakt, "An Ancient and Proven Way to Improve Memorization."

37. Fant, "Memory," 331–32.

38. In the excellent (and exhaustive) *Concise Encyclopedia of Preaching*, the Memory Palace does not receive so much as a passing reference in the article on "Memory," much less an article of its own.

39. Foer, *Moonwalking with Einstein*, 10.

40. Throughout this book, I will use the terms method of loci and Memory Palace nearly interchangeably. Strictly speaking, the former connotes more the process, whereas the latter connotes more the product. Nevertheless, in the literature they are for all practical purposes synonyms. Other terms that will be introduced in turn include *Memoria* and the Art of Memory.

origins and/or dubious value ("Why in the world do I remember the '90s jingle for pizza bagels?"). For Augustine, though, the memory is not an attic; it's a *palace*:

> I will pass then beyond this power of my nature also, rising by degrees unto Him Who made me. And I come to the fields and spacious palaces of my memory, where are the treasures of innumerable images, brought into it from things of all sorts perceived by the senses. There is stored up, whatsoever besides we think, either by enlarging or diminishing, or any other way varying those things which the sense hath come to; and whatever else hath been committed and laid up, which forgetfulness hath not yet swallowed up and buried. When I enter there, I require what I will to be brought forth, and something instantly comes; others must be longer sought after, which are fetched, as it were, out of some inner receptacle; others rush out in troops, and while one thing is desired and required, they start forth, as who should say, "Is it perchance I?" These I drive away with the hand of my heart, from the face of my remembrance; until what I wish for be unveiled, and appear in sight, out of its secret place. Other things come up readily, in unbroken order, as they are called for; those in front making way for the following; and as they make way, they are hidden from sight, ready to come when I will. All which takes place when I repeat a thing by heart.[41]

Fast forward some fifteen hundred years. Sir Arthur Conan Doyle's brilliant detective Sherlock Holmes is remarkable in many ways, but not least his ability to recall with stunning rapidity and accuracy a clue or piece of information from his memory. In a thrilling scene from the critically acclaimed BBC adaptation of the mysteries, we witness the master at work.[42] Sherlock has just been shot point blank, and time slows down as he suddenly must determine what to do to save his own life. In a flash Holmes is

---

41. St. Augustine, *Confessions*, 10.8

42. In the episode entitled "His Last Vow," from series 3 of the BBC's *Sherlock*. This episode has a further twist, as Sherlock's nemesis also makes use of the Memory Palace technique.

exploring what he call his "mind palace": an intricate collection of data laid out like furniture in a mansion of many rooms.[43] Quickly, practically instantaneously, Holmes searches through his mind palace for just the bit of info he needs—in this case, a quick survival tactic. He retrieves it, performs the requisite intervention, and the show goes on. Meanwhile, the viewer is left to marvel at Sherlock's magnificent mind.

What Augustine, with his "vast palaces of memory," and Sherlock, with his "mind palace," are both harkening back to is an ancient, time-tested method of learning by heart. Variously known as the method of loci, Memory Palace, or Art of Memory, it was developed by the ancient Greeks some 400 years before Christ and continued in common use by rhetors of all kinds for more than two millennia. In a nutshell, the method is a mnemonic technique using locations (*loci*) and images (*imagines*) or, otherwise put, Places and Pictures.[44]

First, the speaker thinks of a familiar location, or Place: a childhood home, workplace floor, or even a neighborhood block. Any place that she can recall and retrace without effort. Second, the speaker associates or "translates" the various and sundry points, arguments, or sections of the oration (be it a speech, sermon, toast, etc.) into concrete Pictures. For example, if in the introduction (classically known as the *exordium*) of his closing arguments a lawyer wanted to recount his client's alibi—he was in fact bowling at Featherstone Lanes—he might conjure in his Memory Palace the defendant, adorned with feathers, dropping a bowling ball on his toe.[45] Later, in his refutation of the prosecution's arguments (the *refutatio*) the lawyer might want to point out contradictions in the accuser's testimony—"Was the murder

43. Zielinski, "The Secret of Sherlock's Mind Palace."

44. Throughout this book, Places and Pictures will be capitalized in order to denote the specific Latin vocabulary of the Memory Palace: *loci* and *imagines*, respectively. The Latin terms will themselves occasionally be used as well. More general terms such as "locations" and "images" will be used more loosely and not capitalized.

45. As will be discussed later, the ancients advise that the more ridiculous the image the better.

weapon a candlestick or a revolver, Miss Scarlet?"—by imagining her as conjoined twins, bopping one another over the head with the respective implements. And so on. Finally, the Pictures are arranged throughout (or along) the chosen Place. For example, our lawyer could place his feathered friend in the entrance to his home (that is, the "introduction" of the house) and the irate twins in a subsequent room, such as the kitchen—with other Pictures filling in along the way. Then, in order to recall his closing arguments, the lawyer simply "walks through" the Memory Palace in his mind as he speaks: "In the first place . . ." The end product is thus something like a three-dimensional, virtual reality outline that can be experienced and employed in real time.

In recent years, the Memory Palace has experienced something of a renaissance among so-called "memory athletes" and also those who are required to remember vast sums of information, such as medical students.[46] But as Frances Yates reminds us, in her seminal work on the subject, *The Art of Memory*, "The first basic fact which the student of the history of the classical art of memory must remember is that the art belonged to rhetoric as a technique by which the orator could improve his memory, which would enable him to deliver long speeches from memory with unfailing accuracy."[47] And so, in recovering its use for the pulpit we are, in a sense, seeking to bring the Memory Palace back closer to its home.

Outline of the argument

This thumbnail sketch of the method of loci will be substantially expanded upon and applied to preachers in due course. We will briefly outline the argument from here. In Part I, we will do a historical overview of classical rhetoric in general (chapter 1) and *Memoria* and the Memory Palace in particular (chapter 2). As we will see, the art of memory cannot be isolated from its associated constellation of practices known as the "canons of rhetoric." In this

46. See Foer, *Moonwalking*. A Google search retrieves several websites that promote the *method loci*, e.g., https://mullenmemory.com.

47. Yates, *The Art of Memory*, 18.

initial section we will be interacting especially with the Greco-Roman orators Aristotle, Cicero, Quintilian, and the aforementioned anonymous author of the *Rhetorica ad Herennium.*

This historical foundation has interest in its own right for modern preachers, but for the purposes of this study it is especially necessary in preparing for the practical application of Part II. In this latter half of the book, we will take the lessons learned from the historical practice of classical rhetoric and bring them to bear on modern preaching. Chapter 3 will take initial steps toward developing a weekly process for preparing to preach that has as its framework the classical canons, and then in chapter 4 we will focus on the nuts and bolts of the Memory Palace proper. A concluding chapter will assemble the pieces of the argument and demonstrate how preachers can construct their own Memory Palaces.

PART 1:

Classical Rhetoric
and the Memory Palace

Chapter 1

AN OVERVIEW
OF CLASSICAL RHETORIC

What classical rhetoric is
and why preachers today should care about it

THE MEMORY PALACE IS part of the impressive patrimony of classical rhetoric. The phrase "classical rhetoric" may sound a little vague but it in fact has a relatively specific meaning; we can break it down according to its two parts. By *rhetoric* is meant the art of public speaking, or in the words of the Roman orator Quintilian, it is the *bene dicendi scientia:* "the knowledge of speaking well."[1] The *classical* in this phrase refers to this art as it was developed by the ancient Greeks and Romans, going back to the fifth and fourth centuries BC. The main characters are orators such as Plato and Aristotle (from the Greeks), and Cicero and Quintilian (from the Romans). Putting the pieces together, George Kennedy defines classical rhetoric thusly:

> The Greeks gave names to rhetorical techniques, many of which are found all over the world. They organized these techniques into a system which could be taught and learned. What we mean by classical rhetorical theory

1. Quintilian, *Institutio Oratoria* 2.15.34.

is this structured system which describes the universal phenomenon of rhetoric in Greek terms.[2]

Before going forward, some might well ask why we would *want* to attend to the antiquated public speaking techniques of the ancients. In particular, what relevance could this have for contemporary preachers, who are supposedly living in a "visual age" and its surfeit of images?[3] Several responses come to mind. First, in the broadest sense we might invoke Justin Martyr's famous dictum that "whatever things were rightly said among all men, are the property of us Christians."[4] To the extent that classical rhetoric offers helpful insights into the way communication works, and works well, Christians can and should take advantage of it. Second, many of the greatest preachers of the early church not only employed the art of rhetoric in their preaching but were themselves teachers of oratory—Ambrose, Augustine, Chrysostom, and Gregory of Nyssa among them. As David Dunn-Wilson has observed, "For the great preachers [of the early church] who were trained as rhetors, it seemed natural to transfer their skills to the pulpit."[5] And if it is not already a rule of thumb then it should be one, that if it was good enough for Augustine it is good enough for me. Third, granted that we are living in a "post-literate" age, there may be great benefit in attending to the wisdom of our *pre*-literate forebears.[6] For contemporary preachers, an especially fertile source of such ancient wisdom is classical rhetoric. Finally, to the claim that our preaching should be more "image-based," classical rhetoric generally and the Memory Palace in particular relies heavily on the use of images—just not in the simplistic way sometimes advocated nowadays (such as by using PowerPoint slides). Suffice it to say, then, pastors can and should plunder these ancient spoils, accusations of their being outdated or irrelevant aside.

2. Kennedy, *The New Testament and Rhetorical Criticism*, 11.

3. See, e.g., Sweet, *Post-Modern Pilgrims*.

4. Justin Martyr, *Second Apology* §13.

5. Dunn-Wilson, *A Mirror for the Church*, 86.

6. See especially Ong, *Orality and Literacy*. On our post-literate age, see also Postman, *Amusing Ourselves to Death*, and Jensen, *Thinking in Story*.

Now, the ground of classical rhetoric is broad country and other authors are much more capable cartographers.[7] Here we want only to map some general territory that is particularly pertinent to preachers before homing in on the *ars memoriae*, the art of memory. First, we will consider what Aristotle called the "modes of persuasion." Then, we will look at the five "canons" (or parts) of rhetoric as they were taught by classical rhetoricians. This will bring us back finally to a focus on one of those five canons, *Memoria*.

How to move people with words: the three modes of persuasion

After a particularly effective sermon, a parishioner might say to the preacher, "Thank you for your message today. I found it so *moving*." It's a remarkable turn of phrase, when you think about it. Newton would tell us that no one and nothing is moving unless some external force acts upon it. My chair will stay in its same place unless an earthquake or a four-year-old rattles it. The hitter will stay in the batter's box unless and until a pitch comes in too close. Your coffee will stay situated on the desk until you need another sip of caffeine. Try to command the coffee into your mouth, though, and you will stay thirsty—not to mention drowsy. We do not normally think of words as being such an "external force."

Our grateful parishioner is not speaking nonsense, however. Experience, as well as Scripture, would attest that not only brute force can move someone; so, too, can speech.[8] This is what Aristotle is getting at when he defines rhetoric as "in any given case the

7. See especially Kennedy, *Classical Rhetoric and Its Christian and Secular Tradition from Ancient to Modern Times*, and Corbett, *Classical Rhetoric for the Modern Student*. In order to get a big-picture handle on the field, as well as find a helpful glossary of terms, one might also look at the Silva Rhetoricae ("Forest of Rhetoric") hosted by the Brigham Young University department of rhetoric: http://rhetoric.byu.edu/forest.htm.

8. As my focus here is on rhetoric, I will set aside concern for what Aristotle calls "external" (*atechnoi*) modes of persuasion: coercive threats, contracts, etc. (*Ars Rhetorica* 1355b.)

available means of persuasion." Otherwise put, rhetoric is how to move people—with *words*. And according to Aristotle, the means for effecting this movement are chiefly three:

> Of the modes of persuasion furnished by the spoken word there are three kinds. The first kind depends on the *personal character* of the speaker; the second on putting the audience into a certain *frame of mind*; the third on the proof, or apparent proof, provided by *the words of the speech itself*.[9]

These three kinds are known as, respectively, *ethos, pathos,* and *logos*.[10] First, the speaker persuades by means of their *ethos*, Aristotle says, "when the speech is so spoken as to make us think him credible."[11] On the one hand, *ethos* is established before a word comes out of the speaker's mouth; the expression "their reputation precedes them" gets at this notion. This is why a keynote speaker is introduced with his resume and why brands covet celebrity endorsements. *Ethos* deals in authority, answering the question in the audience's mind—even before a word is uttered—"Why should I listen to you?" (Whether the ability to dunk a basketball makes one an authority on, say, pharmaceuticals is open for debate.) On the other hand, *ethos* can also be established by a speaker in the act of speaking itself. Indeed, Aristotle suggests this is the more appealing aspect of *ethos*, if not more common. From this perspective, *ethos* comes from the competence, confidence, and gravitas of the speaker. When the crowds hail Jesus because "he was teaching them as one who had authority, and not as their scribes" (Matt 7:29), they are responding principally to his *ethos* in this sense. This is also the mode of persuasion most germane to our concerns about memory; more on this presently.

---

9. Aristotle, *Ars Rhetorica* 1356a. Kennedy (*Classical Rhetoric*, 82), notes that these three correspond to the three consistent parts of any speech-act: speaker, audience, and speech.

10. Note that these are not a prescribed order. *Pathos* may just as likely provide a closing appeal as be part of the body of an oration.

11. Aristotle, *Ars Rhetorica* 1.2§4.

Second, the speaker persuades with *pathos*, an appeal to the emotions. Aristotle remarks, having in mind the infamous Sophists of his day, that "it is towards producing these effects . . . that present-day writers on rhetoric direct the whole of their efforts."[12] We could hardly disagree in our own time. Some years back, when a best-selling memoir was discredited as an almost complete fabrication, a certain popular television host defended it on account of the legitimacy of its "underlying message."[13] Maudlin novels or romantic comedies might also come to mind. Abuses and manipulations of the emotions aside, however, *pathos* is a powerful tool of persuasion.[14] The authoritative speaker who can also tug on the heart strings, as we say, is much nearer to moving people than the dry lecturer whose speech is merely accurate.

Third and finally, Aristotle tell us that we as speakers persuade with *logos* (an appeal to reason) "when we have proved a truth or an apparent truth by means of the persuasive *arguments* suitable to the case in question" (my emphasis).[15] Airtight arguments and satisfying syllogisms—"enthymemes" in the rhetoric vernacular—are the domain of *logos*. Aristotle clearly regards *logos* as the superior form of proof, and that every speech ought to rise or fall solely on its logical merits—and many preachers would surely agree. Is it not enough that our sermons are true and logical for people to believe them? In many cases, sad to say, the answer is no. Nevertheless, for preachers of the word, *logos* will always be the *sine qua non* of faithful proclamation.

In any given speech, sermon, or rhetorical event of various kinds, one of these modes of persuasion may suffice. The parent's authority might be sufficient to persuade his teenager to clean her

12. Aristotle, *Ars Rhetorica* 1.2§5.

13. CNN.com, "Winfrey stands behind 'Pieces' author." Winfrey later retracted her defense.

14. In *The Righteous Mind*, 32–60, Jonathan Haidt makes a compelling case that the emotions are themselves are elements of logic (or rationality) via intuition. In this sense, persuasive appeals to *pathos* are not illogical or anti-logical but rather directed toward the more visceral logic of the sentiments—what Haidt calls "the elephant."

15. Aristotle, *Ars Rhetorica* 1.2§11.

room (though that's doubtful). The slick commercial might get me to buy a new car simply by stirring up certain emotions. Or the unadorned professor might persuade her student to embrace supply-side economics solely by the force of her logic. We are going to focus on a single one of these three modes, *ethos*, as it pertains to our concerns about memorization. Needless to say, though, the most potent oratory will tie together all three—the rhetorical "hat trick," if you will.

Memory and Ethos

We observed in the Introduction that preaching with notes creates a credibility problem. From the perspective of Aristotle's modes of persuasion, then, reading a sermon or even working from an outline is primarily an *ethos* issue. But why is this? Data on the role of extemporaneous speaking in establishing *ethos* is scant, but insights from other fields for which public speaking is essential may offer some clues. So let us briefly consider a couple of contemporary heirs of the rhetorical tradition—stage entertainers and a secular equivalent of preachers—to attempt to make some analogous connections to preaching.

The Millionaire Magician: Scripts disrupt connection

Steve Cohen is known as "the millionaire's magician." His career has been built on persuading people to believe the unbelievable and to trust the incredible. Who better, then, to convey the importance of establishing *ethos*? Though it does not use the Greek concept, Cohen's book *Win the Crowd* is essentially an extended treatise on creating credibility and securing a sympathetic ear from your audience.[16]

Cohen writes, "It boils down to being genuine. People want to feel important; they want to know that they are not just another audience." He recounts a conversation he had with the famous

16. Cohen, *Win the Crowd.*

television magician David Blaine. Blaine commended Cohen on his magic, but criticized him on his delivery. "Don't prepare what you are going to say," Blaine insisted. "People should feel like you're talking to them for the first time."[17] Blaine was overstating his case; magicians (and preachers) cannot neglect preparation. The more important point that Cohen gleaned from this encounter, however, was the need to connect with his audience and not mechanically utter prescribed lines. "Let your script drop away and look at your audience dead in the eyes," Cohen writes. "When you consciously recognize that there are live people in front of you, the words come out sounding much fresher."[18] In other words, memory facilitates connection—the most potent power of *ethos*.

TED talkers: Scripts kill charisma

While there is plenty of hand-wringing from American pastors that fewer and fewer people are in the pews to hear their preaching, it is not the case that oratory as such has fallen out of favor. On the contrary, arguably more people than ever are listening with rapt attention to eighteen-minute monologues—it's just not necessarily on Sunday morning, or at least Sunday morning at your local congregation.

TED (short for Technology, Education, and Design) is a non-profit that's "devoted to spreading ideas."[19] The primary way that TED has done this over the last thirty years or so is through succinct, eighteen-minute (or less) messages. What started as an annual, one-off conference in California has now spawned offshoot gatherings around the world and the extraordinarily popular website and podcast. Though more recent data is not available, five years ago TED had already commemorated its one-billionth viewing online.[20]

17. Cohen, *Win the Crowd*, 70.

18. Cohen, *Win the Crowd*, 70.

19. "About," at TED.com, https://www.ted.com/about/our-organization.

20. "TED reaches its billionth video view," https://blog.ted.com/ted-reaches-its-billionth-video-view/.

Unsurprisingly, this popularity has garnered attention from researchers. Carmine Gallo is a "communication coach" and the author of *Talk Like TED*.[21] He evaluated hundreds of TED talks and interviewed many of the most popular speakers. While not addressing the role of memory specifically, Gallo speaks to the importance of "internalizing" one's message in a way that jibes with our definition of preaching by heart. "Practice relentlessly and internalize your content," he writes, "so that you can deliver the presentation as comfortably as having a conversation with a close friend."[22]

Like Cohen, Gallo does not use Aristotle's technical vocabulary. He nevertheless speaks to the importance of *ethos* when he writes that "true persuasion occurs only after you have built an emotional rapport with your listeners and have gained their trust." A key element to building this rapport, he says, is that your delivery comports with your message. "If your voice, gestures, and body language are incongruent with your words," Gallo writes, "your listeners will distrust your message. It's the equivalent of having a Ferrari (a magnificent story) without knowing how to drive (delivery)."[23] This is certainly convicting for us preachers, who profess to carry "the greatest story ever told."

Vanessa Van Edwards is lead investigator at Science of People, a human behavior research lab.[24] Edwards and her researchers wanted to uncover what makes for the most people viewing and hearing TED talks, and took a slightly more scientific tack than Gallo. Her team systematically viewed and graded the various speakers for their charisma, credibility, and intelligence. The greatest finding from their research was that viewers felt a relational connection with speakers *just as much with sound as on mute*. In other words, in terms of the speakers' *ethos*, more important than *content* was *comportment*. Van Edwards writes,

21. Gallo, *Talk Like TED*.
22. Gallo, *Talk Like TED*, 75.
23. Gallo, *Talk Like TED*, 76.
24. "Science of People," www.scienceofpeople.com.

This means we rate someone's charisma, credibility and intelligence based on nonverbal signals. This is surprising—we want people to focus on our words, but this experiment is no different from previous research. Studies have found that 60 to 93% of our communication is nonverbal. Over and over again we find that how we say something is more important than what we say.[25]

We who would follow in the tradition of St. Paul, who proclaimed the gospel "in weakness and in fear and much trembling," will no doubt want to carefully qualify Van Edwards's broad statements. Nevertheless, her bottom line is worth noting. "Scripts kill your charisma," she writes. "[TED] speakers who told stories, ad libbed and even yelled at the audience . . . captivated the audience's imagination and attention."[26] *Ethos* is more firmly established by the speaker who's not just reading (be it from the page or from the "teleprompter in the mind"), but relating.

Modes of Persuasion: Conclusion

Preachers know intuitively what we have now heard, not only from the master of ancient rhetoric but also from modern practitioners of the art of persuasion: the more effectively that the message is internalized, and so able to be spoken by heart, the more credible is its delivery. If preachers would enhance their *ethos*, in other words, they ought to take to heart the sentiment of that Collect and "read, mark, learn, and *inwardly digest* God's holy word."[27]

25. Van Edwards, "5 Secrets of a Successful TED Talk."

26. Van Edwards, "5 Secrets of a Successful TED Talk."

27. One caveat may be in order: preachers can of course still establish their *ethos* apart from preaching by heart—most especially by the conformity of their lives to their message. "Keep a close watch on yourself and on the teaching," reads 1 Timothy. "Persist in this, for by so doing you will save both yourself and your hearers" (1 Tim 4:16). And as Aristotle says, "It is not true . . . that the personal goodness revealed by the speaker contributes nothing to his power of persuasion; on the contrary, his character may almost be called the most effective means of persuasion he possesses" (Aristotle, *Ars Rhetorica* I.2). So let it be said: note-free preaching is not the only means to building *ethos*.

And while speaking by heart is not the only means to establish credibility it is nevertheless a potent one, and one that preachers can develop using the well-worn tools of classical rhetoric. Let's turn, then, to those tools—what the ancients called the "canons" of rhetoric, including *Memoria*.

The orator's toolbox: the canons of rhetoric

The journey from idea to utterance, from discovery to oratory, need not be a haphazard one, according to the luminaries of classical rhetoric. "All the activity and ability of an orator falls into five divisions," said Cicero.[28] And these five divisions, or "canons," can provide a kind of roadmap for the journey of the orator—preachers included. In this section I will provide a brief overview of the canons before in the next chapter narrowing our attention to what was traditionally the fourth canon, *Memoria*, and the practice of the Memory Palace.

Inventio (Discovery)

If rhetoric is the practice of moving people with words, first you need some words with which to do it. You need *material*, one might say. This is the first stop on the journey of crating an oration, the first canon of rhetoric: Invention (*Inventio*). It's sometimes called "Discovery," and this perhaps better conveys both the etymology and the actual process of this stage: you are not so much *coming up* with something to talk about; you are *coming upon* it. "Invention," says Cicero in his treatise of the same name, "is the discovery of valid or seemingly valid arguments to render one's cause plausible."[29]

One typical way in which classical rhetoricians discovered and developed material in the Invention stage was through "topics" (*topoi* in Greek, *loci* in Latin). In a *tour de force* chapter in

---

28. Cicero, *De Oratore* I.XXXI §142–43

29. Cicero, *De Inventione* I.VII §9.

his *Ars Rhetorica*, Aristotle adduces twenty-eight different "commonplaces" (as they came to be called). Space does not allow for an in-depth exploration of *topoi* here, but allow me to highlight a few that are also familiar from the Scriptures.[30]

Consider the commonplace of *a fortiori* argument. "The principle here," Aristotle says, "is that if a quality does not in fact exist where it is *more* likely to exist, it clearly does not exist where it is *less* likely."[31] You might call it the "(how) much more" topic. This line of argument is clearly well represented in the New Testament. For example, Jesus admonishes the disciples, "What father among you, if his son asks for a fish, will instead of a fish give him a serpent; or if he asks for an egg, will give him a scorpion? If you then, who are evil, know how to give good gifts to your children, *how much more* will the heavenly Father give the Holy Spirit to those who ask him!" (Luke 11:11–13).

Another commonplace is that of defining one's terms, to "get at its essential meaning, and then use the result when reasoning on the point at issue."[32] This is a favorite method of 1 John. "In this is love," the epistle reads, "not that we have loved God but that he loved us and sent his Son to be the propitiation for our sins." And then the corollary: "Beloved, if God so loved us, we also ought to love one another" (1 John 4:10–11).

Finally, we might recall the cause/effect line of argument. "By proving the cause," the philosopher writes, "you at once prove the effect, and conversely nothing can exist without its cause."[33] A parade example of this is in Romans 5. Paul states the remarkable assertion, "We rejoice in our sufferings." Inevitably, the hearer of this wants more explanation, which Paul offers by reasoning from suffering's effects: "Knowing that suffering produces endurance, and endurance produces character, and character produces hope, and hope does not put us to shame, because God's love has been

30. For more on *topoi* in the Scriptures, see Small, "The Use of Rhetorical *Topoi* in the Characterization of Jesus in the Book of Hebrews."

31. Aristotle, *Ars Rhetorica* II.23 §4.

32. Aristotle, *Ars Rhetorica* II.23 §7.

33. Aristotle, *Ars Rhetorica* II.23 §24.

poured into our hearts" (Rom 5:3-5). One trait tumbles out after another in succession.

As with each of these canons of rhetoric, much more could of course be said. The author of the *Rhetorica ad Herennium* calls Invention "the most difficult part of rhetoric."[34] Suffice it say for our purposes, however, that Invention is the stage for developing the raw material of your speech. For a preacher, this will be the time of translating from the original languages, reading commentaries, assembling ideas about the passage or theme to be preached on, searching out illustrative material, and so on.[35] Once all this is out on the table, so to speak, now it's time to give it order and form.

Dispositio (Arrangement)

If Invention asks, "What do I have to say?," Arrangement (*Dispositio*) asks, "How can I best order what I have to say?" "It is through Arrangement," writes the author of the *Rhetorica ad Herennium*, "that we set in order the topics we have invented so that there may be a definite place for each in the delivery."[36] Rather than slapping together the parts of a speech piecemeal, this second canon encourages the orator to piece them together with intentionality.

In his *Phaedrus*, Plato uses an engaging and memorable analogy that illustrates this task of Arrangement.[37] Think of a butcher carving up a chicken, he has Socrates saying. A clumsy butcher (or yours truly on Thanksgiving Day) mutilates the bird. He hacks the thing all to pieces, cutting against the grain of the meat and sawing through bone. The clever butcher, on the other hand, recognizes that the chicken has natural carving places. He deftly divides the bones at their joins, cuts the meat with the grain, and ends up with a much more satisfying meal.

---

34. Pseudo-Cicero, *Rhetorica ad Herennium* III.VIII §15.

35. In chapter 3 below we will apply the insights of each of the canons to the process of sermon preparation.

36. Pseudo-Cicero, *Rhetorica ad Herennium* III.IX §16.

37. Plato, *Phaedrus* 265e.

I suppose it does not sound quite right to say that preachers want to "butcher" their sermons, but you see the point of Plato's analogy. The goal in Arrangement is to divide and order the movements of the message such that it flows naturally for the hearers and that the different parts of the sermon fall satisfyingly into place. David Schmitt, professor of homiletics at Concordia Seminary, speaks in this vein of the importance of sermon structures, which he defines as "the purposeful ordering of ideas and experiences in the sermon."[38] Such structures are essentially tools of Arrangement.

Ultimately, Arrangement helps to facilitate the function of the proclamation. It is hard enough to follow a disjointed, garbled argument when it is written on the page; you might be able to re-read a paragraph or two, and even then struggle to find the thread. When a speech or sermon is disorganized, however, the poor hearers have almost no hope of following along. At best, they'll look for a little nugget of wisdom, knowing that that sermon lacks a larger coherence. On the contrary, a well-ordered sermon—like a well-butchered bird—is a service to the recipients and better ensures that the message hits home. Or as Pseudo-Cicero puts it, changing metaphors once more, "This Arrangement of topics in speaking, like the arraying of soldiers in battle, can readily bring victory."[39]

Elocutio (Style)

It is probably fair to say that when many people hear "rhetoric" they think of its third canon, Style (*elocutio*). Cicero defines it as "the fitting of the proper language to the invented matter."[40] Here one might also invoke Francis Bacon's definition of rhetoric generally as "the application of reason to imagination for the better moving of the will."[41] The heart of composition, Style employs ornamenta-

---

38. Schmitt, "Sermon Structures."
39. Pseudo-Cicero, *Rhetorica ad Herennium* III.X §18.
40. Cicero, *De Inventione* I.VII §9.
41. Bacon, *De Augmentis* II.XVIII §2.

tion and orchestration in language in order to engage not only the mind but the heart—always, again, toward the goal of persuasion. In this way, Style is closely allied with *Pathos* as discussed above: if a speaker would stir the emotions, she needs to delight and not merely inform.[42]

It is beyond the scope of this study to cover Style in depth.[43] It is worthwhile, however, to address the principal danger of Style—one that may tempt some to discount rhetoric altogether. We might call this danger the Sophist's Error: all Style, no substance. The Sophists, whom we have alluded to already, were notorious for peddling persuasive oratory that might titillate the ears but did not edify the mind or soul. Well-sounding words that are at best hollow and at worst deceptive.[44]

Preachers tend to be especially sensitive to the Sophist's Error, influenced by St. Paul's words in 1 Corinthians: "And I, when I came to you, brothers, did not come proclaiming to you the testimony of God with lofty speech or wisdom. For I decided to know nothing among you except Jesus Christ and him crucified" (1 Cor 2:1–2). St. Paul's well-reasoned and moving arguments in his letters to Corinth and elsewhere—that is, his effective rhetoric—seem to contradict his expressed sentiment; as Cicero once said of Plato, "It was when making fun of orators that he himself seemed to be the consummate orator."[45] Be that as it may, Paul's point is well taken. In his day as in our own, there are many who sacrifice substance on the altar of Style—whether it be websites proffering "clickbait" articles or preachers with shallow self-help teaching.

So yes, the Sophist's Error is real, and it is a real danger. Preachers should not for that reason attempt to eschew Style altogether; indeed, "plain" is its own sort of Style. The goal is to wed

42. See also Cicero's *officia oratoris* ("duties of the orator"): *probare* ("to prove"), *delectare* ("to delight"), and *flectere* ("to stir"). *Orator* XXI.69.

43. The modern standard is still *The Elements of Style* by William Strunk and E. B. White. See also, more recently, Steven Pinker, *The Sense of Style*.

44. It could be argued that much modern advertising is an example of the Sophist's Error.

45. Cited in Church, "Rhetorical Structure and Design in Paul's Letter to Philemon," 17.

Style *with* substance, form *with* content. Once again, Cicero may have put it best: "Wisdom without eloquence does too little to benefit states, but eloquence without wisdom does too much harm and is never advantageous."[46] When both are held together, Style is a potent part of persuasion.[47]

Pronuntiatio (Delivery)

We will soon turn our full attention to the fourth canon of rhetoric, Memory, so let's jump ahead briefly to consider what is traditionally the fifth and final canon, Delivery (*Pronuntiatio*). Delivery is, as we say, where the rubber hits the road. All the hard work of developing the message can founder if the delivery is wanting. "It matters less what sort of things we have composed within ourselves, than how we utter them," says Quintilian, making the obvious but oft overlooked point, "because people are affected according to what they hear."[48]

Delivery was traditionally divided into two parts, voice and gesture.[49] How you carry yourself, and how your voice carries. While we tend to think of the sermon as what has been written beforehand, that is really only a piece—albeit an important, indispensable piece—of the puzzle. When all of those pieces are in place, though, the result is impactful oratory: "Indeed, since words are very powerful by themselves, and the voice adds its own contribution to the content, and gestures and movements have a meaning, then, when they all come together, the result must be perfection."[50] It is worth underscoring once more that, though our study here is to focus on Memory (and just as we saw above regarding the modes of persuasion), *all* the canons of rhetoric are important.

46. Cicero, *De Inventione* I.I.

47. Augustine picks up on this line of argumentation in *De Doctrina Christiana (On Christian Teaching)*.

48. Quintilian, *Institutio Oratoria* XI.3 §2.

49. See, e.g., Pseudo-Cicero, *Rhetorica ad Herennium* III §20.

50. Quintilian, *Institutio Oratoria* XI.3 §9.

The seriousness with which the Athenian orator Demosthenes took Delivery is legendary and illustrates how it was regarded among the ancients. Sounding like a modern realtor, when asked what the three most important rules in the business of oratory were he responded, "Delivery, Delivery, Delivery."[51] According to Plutarch, Demosthenes would bone up on his skills by reciting speeches with pebbles in his mouth (to help with his enunciation) and holding forth as he hustled up and down hills.[52] Whether most pastors today could even run up a hill, let alone while preaching, is debatable. But I digress.

It is worth noting that the Greek word for the canon of Delivery was *hypokrisis*. Initially it had the neutral meaning of "acting," but of course Jesus gave it the more negative cast. This verbal coincidence again cautions against the Sophist's Error, however. Paul's point to the Corinthians, mentioned above, was that he was not being showy or manipulative. The goal of employing not only Memory but all the tools of rhetoric is to preach persuasively by heart—not to put on a show or try to elicit an emotional response. To be sure, as Paul wrote to the Philippians in a verse already quoted, "Whether in pretense or in truth, Christ is proclaimed, and in that I rejoice" (Phil 1:18). Needless to say, though, that is not a license for gross hypocrisy. "If Delivery has this power to produce anger, tears, or anxiety over matters which we know to be fictitious and unreal," said Quintilian, "how much more powerful must it be when we really believe!"[53] So it ought to be for preachers.

51. Quintilian, *Institutio Oratoria* XI.3 §7.

52. Plutarch, *Life of Demosthenes* XI.1–2.

53. Quintilian, *Institutio Oratoria* XI.3 §5.

Overview of Classical Rhetoric—Recap

- Classical rhetoric is the art of public speaking as it was developed by the ancient Greeks and Romans
- Three modes of persuasion:
  1. *Ethos*—the personal character and credibility of the speaker
  2. *Logos*—the inner reasonableness of the speech
  3. *Pathos*—the emotional resonance of the speech
- Five "canons" (or parts) of rhetoric
  1. Discovery (*Inventio*)—gathering sources and arguments for the speech
  2. Arrangement (*Dispositio*)—the purposeful structuring of ideas and experiences in the speech
  3. Style (*Elocutio*)— "the fitting of the proper language to the invented matter" (Cicero)
  4. Memory (*Memoria*)—see next chapter
  5. Delivery (*Pronuntiatio*)—speaking effectively and persuasively

Chapter 2

MEMORIA
AND THE MEMORY PALACE

The birth of the Memory Palace

"YOU NEED TO *REMEMBER!*" The officer pounded the table for emphasis. The man he was speaking to stared at the floor bewilderingly.

"I—it's just—there were so many people," the man said. It wasn't like him to be at a loss for words.

"That's just the point," said the officer. "Dozens of people—family, friends—are counting on you. Your memory of that party is the difference between their peace and their pain."

The party in question had started innocently enough. It was a grand gala, hosted at the mansion of a town dignitary in honor of the local hero—a boxer who had claimed the heavyweight belt. (This was many years ago, when boxing still carried some cultural cachet.) The victory celebration continued into the wee hours of the night. The music and the dancing and the feasting kept everyone in reverie. Enough so that they didn't notice the crack that was creeping across the aged ceiling like a snake slithering through the reeds.

Part of the entertainment for the evening was the hotshot poet laureate of the area. He had one job. The dignitary had asked him to prepare and deliver a special ode to the boxer (no Simon and Garfunkel covers allowed). The poet agreed, but being a true *artiste* he wasn't about to be constrained by the conventions of his bourgeois host. He took to the makeshift stage at the front of the banquet hall and surveyed the room. The guests were all in predictable places. There, off to the left, was the crooked prosecutor with his paramour in the dim light. The aldermen all sat at the same table in the back corner by the buffet line, stuffing their faces and sipping their gin. And front and center was of course the boxer and his entourage.

The poet watched some plaster pirouette from the ceiling and sighed something like a prayer. Finally, he intoned. He briefly praised the boxer, beholding the self-satisfied grins of his crowd. But then he promptly steered a course into his own arcane idiom (there may have been some reference to Castor and Pollux). It all came off like a T. S. Eliot poem without the footnotes. A spattering of applause greeted its merciful end. As our poet slipped outside for a post-performance smoke, muttering to himself about the Philistines at the party, the dignitary buttonholed him.

"You'll only be getting half your fee," he said, "since we only understood half your blathering."

"Keep your filthy cash," the poet responded. "You'll need it to fix up this dump." And he stomped out the back door as the party resumed behind him.

He had hardly gotten beyond the no-smoking halo surrounding the building when the crash came. It started with a wheezing, groaning *craaaack*. Then a succession of pops lit out as the bolts broke free from their sockets. And like the planned implosion of some blighted, inner-city tower, the mansion collapsed in on itself. The poet looked on in disbelief as the dignitary, the attorney, the town hero, and all the rest were in a moment flattened like grass beneath a drowsy Saint Bernard. In a daze, the poet wandered back to his apartment and fell into his bed, hoping to forget a horrific evening.

The next day a knock came at the door. It was the officer. "Look, I was just the entertainment," the poet protested through a crack in the doorway. "I had nothing to do with the crash."

"No, you didn't," the officer said. "Everyone knew that old house wasn't long for this world; it was foolish to host the party there. But now we need your help."

The officer sat the poet down and explained to him that he was the only person who came out of the mansion that night alive. The bodies had been mangled beyond all recognition, and these were the days before anyone could be identified through dental records or fingerprints. Neither was there any guestbook to go on, much less a seating assignment. Now anxious citizens wanted to know if their family or friends were there, and if so, which body to bury where—the devastation was that complete.

At first the poet protested. "Hey, there were a lot of people in that room," he says, "and I was hardly there for a few minutes before they ran me out." He lit a cigarette.

The officer dropped his fist on the table, and the poet dropped his cigarette. "You need to *remember!*"

The poet sighed and leaned back in his chair, closing his eyes. Suddenly the faces started to come back to him as he walked the room in his mind. The prosecutor popping olives into his mistress's mouth. The city council stuffing themselves with third helpings. And of course the boxer and his lackeys laughing at all his bad jokes. A smirk came across the poet's face. He opened his eyes and sat forward in his chair.

"Give me a pad of paper," he said.

* * *

Such is the (admittedly embellished) anecdote that, legend has it, gave birth to the Memory Palace. The poet Simonides was invited by Scopus of Thessaly, a wealthy nobleman, to compose an encomium for a great banquet—some say in honor of the host, some say in honor of a victorious boxer; the details differ among the ancients' accounts.[1] The moral of the story, however, is constant. As Cicero puts it:

> Simonides was enabled by his recollection of the place in which each of them had been reclining at table to identify them for separate interment; and ... this circumstance suggested to him the discovery of the truth that the best aid to clearness of memory consists in orderly arrangement. He inferred that persons desiring to train this faculty must select localities and form mental images of the facts they wish to remember and store those images in the localities, with the result that the arrangement of the localities will preserve the order of the facts, and the images of the facts will designate the facts themselves, and we shall employ the localities and images respectively as a wax writing tablet and the letters written on it.[2]

This origin story for the art of memory was evidently standard among teachers and practitioners of rhetoric in the ancient world. Frances Yates writes, "One may perhaps conjecture that [the Simonides anecdote] formed the normal introduction to the section on artificial memory in a textbook on rhetoric."[3] It is not clear, though, whether the account was regarded as a fanciful tale or a reliable testimony.

These dubious historical origins of the art of memory notwithstanding, the Simonides story is a helpful entree into our discussion of the Memory Palace as it was understood and taught within classical rhetoric: a system of remembering—particularly for orators—that relied on sites and symbols, locations and images. In this chapter, we will first touch on the place of memory within the five canons of rhetoric, including what the ancients regarded as the two kinds of memory. Then, we will get into the Memory Palace proper, its elements and practice, and see how the Simonides story illustrates it at work. Finally, we will consider an

---

1. Cicero's account is the most complete, in *De Oratore* II.351–54. Quintilian included the detail about the boxer in *Instiutio Oratoria* 11.2 §11–14.

2. *De Oratore* II.354.

3. Yates, *The Art of Memory*, 42.

objection that may be raised by contemporary preachers, and that was already being leveled against the art of memory two millennia ago.

Memory among the canons of rhetoric

Memoria, the process of learning your speech by heart so that you can deliver it without the use of notes, was traditionally reckoned fourth in the order of the canons of rhetoric. This spot may belie its importance,[4] though classical rhetoricians did use a pair of images to describe *Memoria* that underscore its integral place within rhetoric generally: Memory as *foundation* and *guardian.* "All these [canons of rhetoric]," says Cicero, "are but parts of a building as it were." *Inventio* (Invention) furnishes the building, *Pronuntiatio* (Delivery) is like the windows ("that which gives the building light"), and so on. Where in this building, then, does *Memoria* fit? The walls, the doors, the shingles? No: "the *foundation* (*fundamentum*) is Memory."[5] According to Cicero, it is *Memoria* that allows the structure of the speech to stand at all. All the other rhetorical work is in vain, like a beautiful house built on sand, if the oratory is forgotten when the time comes for it to be delivered. Thus, though it may be fourth in order, *Memoria* is in many respects primary in importance.

The other two main characters in our account, Quintilian and the author of the *Ad Herennium,* draw on a similar image but put *Memoria* in a different place—albeit one of arguably equal import. "Memory," wrote Quintilian, is "the *common guardian,* as it were, of all [the canons]."[6] In a way that calls Cicero's argument to mind, he says that we may adequately discover material

---

4. That is, unless we are using a baseball analogy and think of *Memoria* as batting clean-up. But by all accounts Cicero did not know the first thing about first base.

5. Cicero, *De Optimo Genere Oratorum* II §5 (my emphasis). NB: we will later tweak the "building" metaphor in describing the process of preparing to preach using the Memory Palace technique.

6. Quintilian, *Institutio Oratoria* 3.3 §7. My emphasis.

(*Inventio*), capably arrange it (*Dispositio*), and colorfully put it into words (*Elocutio*), but all of this is for nought if it is not finally remembered. "Memory in fact embraces everything which has been brought together to contribute to a speech," he writes.[7] Similarly, the author of the *Ad Herennium*, who authored his work some one hundred years before Quintilian, wrote this: "Now let me turn to the treasure-house (*thesaurus*) of the ideas supplied by Invention, to *the guardian of all the parts of rhetoric*, the Memory."[8] If Cicero envisions *Memoria upholding* the speech, these two envision it *protecting* the speech. In both instances, though, the indispensable role played by Memory is apparent.

Some preachers may quibble with this exalted assessment of Memory. From their perspective, Memory might be more like the wallpaper and window dressing than the foundation: nice to have, perhaps, but not necessary. They might even invoke St. Paul: "For no one can lay a foundation[9] other than that which is laid, which is Jesus Christ" (1 Cor 3:11). This is a fair point; we do not want to push the house metaphor for oratory too far. The word of the gospel is forever and always the solid rock upon which we stand. Other preachers, furthermore, might agree that Memory is more fluff than foundation, but not because it conflicts with the content of the proclamation; rather, because to them it seems to be a gift that some have and others do not—like having perfect pitch or being able to pitch perfectly.

Natural and Artificial Memory

As it happens, the ancients wrestled with this same question. Is Memory simply an innate talent? Or can it be taught and trained? On the one hand, we intuitively grasp that it can get better or (more often) worse; that's one reason people will often give for toiling away at crossword puzzles. And yet, on the other hand, it

---

7. Quintilian, *Institutio Oratoria* 3.3 §10.

8. Pseudo-Cicero, *Rhetorica ad Herennium* III §28. My emphasis.

9. In the Latin Vulgate "foundation" is *fundamentum*.

undoubtedly seems to be the case that some people are blessed with better capacities for remembrance and recall than others (think of those whom we regard as having "photographic memories").

It was a commonplace among the ancients to make such a distinction between what they called the "natural" (*naturalis*) and the "artificial" (*artificiosa*). The former was inborn, or "God's gift," as we might say; the latter was cultivated through education and practice. There were, to be sure, some who insisted that the natural was all that was needed. For example, Longinus wrote, "The only art to ensure [sublimity] is to be born to it."[10] Within classical rhetoric, however, there is an emphasis on the artificial, without ignoring the role of the natural. So Quintilian will respond to those who are "all natural": "Well, let them keep their opinion that to be born is enough to make a man an orator; but I hope they will pardon the efforts of those of us who think that nothing comes to perfection unless nature is assisted by art."[11]

The *Ad Herennium* discusses at length the distinction as it pertains to *Memoria* specifically. "The natural memory," the author writes, "is that memory which is imbedded in our minds, born simultaneously with thought. The artificial memory is that memory which is strengthened by a kind of training and system of discipline." Here we see again an affirmation that the natural memory is necessary but not sufficient when it comes to the orator's skills. He goes on:

> But just as in everything else the merit of natural excellence often rivals acquired learning, and art, in its turn, reinforces and develops the natural advantages, so does it happen in this instance. The natural memory, if a person is endowed with an exceptional one, is often like this artificial memory, and this artificial memory, in its turn, retains and develops the natural advantages by a method of discipline. Thus the natural memory must be strengthened by discipline so as to become exceptional, and, on

---

10. Longinus, *De Sublimis* 2.1.
11. Quintilian, *Institutio Oratoria* 11.3 §11.

the other hand, this memory provided by discipline requires natural ability.[12]

To get only slightly ahead of ourselves, if preachers want to be
all that they can be, then they must (to paraphrase 2 Peter) make
every effort to supplement their natural memories with the virtue
of artificial memory. And here, as the essence of the *ars memoriae*,
is where the Memory Palace comes in.

A System of Places and Pictures

Science journalist Austin Frakt had a curious New Year's resolu-
tion. He resolved to devote every walk from his home to the train
for his morning commute to contemplating details of his work, in
the hopes that he might improve his recall of them. Much to his
surprise, so far he has been successful. In a recent article for *The
New York Times* he lays out his strategy:

> Features of certain landmarks—specific houses and
> parks I pass—have become loci for [aspects of my work],
> converted to images and scenes of my own invention. I
> figuratively walk through my work as I literally walk to it.
> For example, I associated an analysis of the time patients
> wait for care with cars waiting at an intersection I cross.[13]

In a nutshell, Frakt has laid out the fundamental elements of
the Memory Palace. As Frances Yates puts it, the Memory Palace is
a "mnemonic of places and images."[14] Or as we have referred to it
for the purposes of this book, a system of Places and Pictures (*loci*
and *imagines*).[15] By tapping into the power of spatial recall and
the mind's attraction to images, Places and Pictures taken together
provide a potent one-two memory punch. And so now we turn to
considering these two elements in detail.

---

12. Pseudo-Cicero, *Rhetorica ad Herennium* III §29.

13. Frakt, "An Ancient and Proven Way to Improve Memorization."

14. Yates, *The Art of Memory*, 18.

15. The Loeb edition of the *Ad Herennium* translates *loci* as "backgrounds."

Places

In his later years, Eugene Pauly could not remember his best friends or which day of the week it was. He didn't recognize photos of his grandchildren. He would rise in the morning to cook himself bacon and eggs, return to bed, and forty minutes later repeat the task. Eugene had experienced viral encephalitis, a condition that decimated his memory. While he was able to stay at home with his wife, Beverly, doctors warned her that she needed to keep a close eye on him at all times lest he wander off and get lost.

One morning the door to their San Diego home was left open, and while Beverly was getting ready for the day Eugene slipped out. Frantic, Beverly began combing the neighborhood: knocking on doors, peeking over fences, asking strangers on the street if they'd seen a man fitting Eugene's description. After searching high and low for a quarter-hour, she hustled back to the house to call the police. But to her great surprise, she returned to find him in his favorite recliner watching the History Channel. When a relieved Beverly asked Eugene where he'd been, he responded that he'd been sitting there watching the television. The pile of pinecones on the end table and his fingers, sticky with sap, betrayed him. Unbeknownst to Eugene, he had been out for a walk around the block.

For some time Eugene and Beverly had gone on daily walks around the neighborhood. The path was imprinted on his mind beneath even his conscious awareness. Thus, while he couldn't remember that he had been out for a morning stroll, he could nevertheless retrace the course effortlessly and make it back safely to his Lazy Boy. Our spatial memory is powerful.[16]

This is the foundational insight of the Memory Palace: humans have a remarkable capacity for spatial memory. As adults, we're able to dazzle our kids with the ability simply to climb in the car and drive to the grandparents' house a half-hour away without so much as consulting a map. (Though the omnipresent GPS is fast removing the wonder of this.) Places and spaces, especially those

16. Eugene Pauly's story is recounted in Duhigg, *The Power of Habit*, 10–11.

in which we live and move and have our being, become part of the backgrounds of our minds. We don't have to think about their existence; they are just *there*. The ancients had an intuitive grasp of this. Quintilian remarked, "Memory can be assisted if localities are impressed upon the mind. Everyone will believe this from his own experience. When we return to a certain place after an interval, we not only recognize it but remember what we did there, persons are recalled, and sometimes even unspoken thoughts come back to mind."[17] The art of memory leverages this human capacity in order to retain and recall information—and especially (at least historically) for the purpose of public speaking.[18]

And so the first step in the method of loci was selecting a Place that would become the setting for one's Memory Palace. The *Ad Herennium* provided some guidance here. "By *loci* I mean such scenes as are naturally or artificially set off on a small scale, complete and conspicuous," it reads, "so that we can grasp and embrace them easily by the natural memory—for example, a house, an intercolumnar space, a recess, an arch, or the like."[19] The idea was that these spaces be both well-known and distinct. A large hall that one is familiar with, for example, may not be suitable as a Place for one's Memory Palace if it lacks distinctive areas or features. Conversely, a detailed mansion would be useless if the orator were unable to retrace its rooms without additional mental strain. The goal was that the *locus*, the Place, of the Memory Palace simply be background. If one has to think about it too much then the method is not working.[20]

The classical writers recommend having, as it were, a storehouse of Places. This is of course mandatory if one is to continue

17. Quintilian, *Institutio Oratoria* 11.2 §17.

18. Recently the art of memory has experienced a modest renaissance among so-called "memory athletes," as documented Joshua Foer in *Moonwalking with Einstein*. The focus of this book, to reiterate, is strictly its use in oratory.

19. Pseudo-Cicero, *Ad Herennium* III §30.

20. Some recent research suggests that *loci* need not be actual places, but may be creations of the imagination. This will be explored further in a later chapter.

adding information *ad infinitum*. If, however, your goals are more modest—to keep the content of a sermon for a single Sunday, for example—you may need only a handful. We will be discussing the practical aspects of this for preachers in a subsequent chapter. For the time being, let it suffice to say that the number of Places needed accords with the amount of information one hopes to retain via the method of loci.

Part and parcel in the use of Places was also Arrangement (*Dispositio*). We spoke above about Arrangement, which is the canon of rhetoric devoted to ordering one's thoughts. Without structure to the orator's speech, the Memory Palace would quickly devolve into a cluttered closet. When the speech, sermon, or address has a clearly delineated structure, though, it can easily be mapped on to a Place. So the *Ad Herennium* notes, "If these [parts of the speech] have been arranged in order, the result will be that, reminded by the images, we can repeat orally what we have committed to the backgrounds (*loci*), proceeding in either direction from any background we please. That is why it also seems best to arrange the backgrounds in a series."[21] Thus we notice once more in passing the necessary integration of all the canons, Memoria included.

Having selected a Place that fits well with the structure of the speech, then, the orator turns to the next task: furnishing the Memory Palace. Here is where the Pictures come in.

Pictures

The Place that the orator of old would use for his Memory Palace was like an empty house: it needed to be furnished. And the furnishings, so to speak, would be the actual content of his speech: the ideas, arguments, stories, and so on that he wished to include. These elements were associated with images, or Pictures, that could be fixed in the memory; as Aristotle had famously asserted,

---

21. Pseudo-Cicero, *Ad Herennium* III §31.

"The soul never thinks without an image."[22] The Memory Palace applies this ancient insight to the practice of speaking by heart. But before we can say more about this process of "translation," so to speak, let's briefly address a pair of possible misunderstandings, one more easily addressed than the other.

The first concerns the nature of the Pictures. When you think of a picture, you generally think of a static image. This is not the idea that the classical orators had in mind for their *imagines*. They were, as Frances Yates notes, *imagines agentes*: "*active* images."[23] Or to use an old-fashioned phrase, these images are "moving pictures." And so when we speak of Pictures throughout this study, bear in mind that they are dynamic portrayals rather than static portraits; the people and props in our Pictures are always *doing* something— often something quite ridiculous (more on that shortly).

The second possible misunderstanding requires a little more explanation. It was raised already by ancient orators, and no doubt would be raised by modern preachers as well: should I strive to memorize my speech word for word? Do I need to turn every last conjunction and clause into a Picture in my Memory Palace? Here, classical rhetoric makes a helpful distinction between Pictures (or likenesses) of the *thing* (*res*) and the *word* (*verbum*). "Likenesses are bound to be of two kinds, one of things, the other of words," reads the *Ad Herennium*. "Likenesses of *things* are formed when we enlist images that present a general view of the matter with which we are dealing; likenesses of *words* are established when the record of each single noun or appellative is kept by an image."[24] Commenting on this, Yates writes, "For the rhetoric student 'things' and 'words' have an absolutely precise meaning in relation to the five parts of the rhetoric . . . *Things* are thus the subject matter of the speech; *words* are the language in which the subject matter is clothed."[25]

22. Aristotle, *De Anima* III, 7, 431a, 14–17.

23. Yates, *The Art of Memory*, 26.

24. Pseudo-Cicero, *Ad Herennium* III §33. For clarity, I've altered the Loeb translation of *res* from "subject matter" to "things."

25. Yates, *The Art of Memory*, 24.

Thus the question: should the orator strive to learn by heart word for word or thing for thing (or "thought for thought")? While the word-for-word approach certainly has value (for example, in memorizing Scripture or poetry), when it comes to crafting their Memory Palaces a "thing-for-thing" approach is sufficient for orators. So Cicero writes:

> A memory for words, which for us is less essential, is given distinctness by a greater variety of images; for there are many words which serve as joints connecting the limbs of the sentence, and these cannot be formed by any use of simile—of these we have to model images for constant employment; but a memory for things is the special property of the orator—this we can imprint on our minds by a skillful arrangement of the several masks that represent them, so that we may grasp ideas by means of images and their order by means of localities.[26]

In other words, the orator needn't trouble him or herself trying to "translate" every last word of the speech into Pictures. This would be both tedious and counter-productive.[27] For most speakers, most of the time, turning things into Pictures is more than enough. So, then, how was this done?

Consider the parade example from the *Ad Herennium* of a lawyer committing to memory the details of a case:

> Often we encompass the record of an entire matter by one notation, a single image. For example, the prosecutor has said that the defendant killed a man by poison, has charged that the motive for the crime was an inheritance, and declared that there are many witnesses and accessories to this act. If in order to facilitate our defense we wish to remember this first point, we shall in our first

26. Cicero, *De Oratore* II.359–60.

27. This is not to say, of course, that it *cannot* be done at certain points in a speech. For example, a preacher may have a carefully worded statement of gospel proclamation that she wants to include at one point in the sermon. There's no reason that can't be made into a portion of the Memory Palace. The point is that to do this with every sentence of the sermon would be unnecessarily onerous.

background form an image of the whole matter. We shall picture the man in question as lying ill in bed, if we know his person. If we do not know him, we shall yet take some one to be our invalid, but not a man of the lowest class, so that he may come to mind at once. And we shall place the defendant at the bedside, holding in his right hand a cup, and in his left tablets, and on the fourth finger a ram's testicles. In this way we can record the man who was poisoned, the inheritance, and the witnesses.[28]

Notice the rather straightforward process used here. Each of the various points of the case are boiled down to a simple image, or Picture. The victim is laid up in a hospital bed, holding a trio of items: a cup, tablets, and, yes, a ram's testicles.[29] Each of these correspond to, and so call to mind, different elements of the case: the means, motive, and witnesses, respectively. By associating abstract ideas with concrete Pictures, the subject matter of the argument is fixed in the memory.

The curious case of the ram's testicles illustrates what was regarded as the key to developing good Pictures. Yates remarks, "This is an example of a classical memory image—consisting of human figures, active, dramatic, striking, with accessories to remind of the whole 'thing' which is being recorded in memory."[30] In other words, the more vivid, strange, and unexpected the better. So the author of the *Ad Herennium* explains, "Now nature herself teaches us what we should do. When we see in everyday life things that are petty, ordinary, and banal, we generally fail to remember them, because the mind is not being stirred by anything novel or marvelous. But if we see or hear something exceptionally base, dishonorable, extraordinary, great, unbelievable, or laughable, that we are likely to remember a long time."[31]

---

28. Pseudo-Cicero, *Ad Herennium* III §33–34.

29. The Latin *testes* is very similar to the word for "witnesses," *testis*. See further in chapter 4 below.

30. Yates, *Art of Memory*, 27.

31. Pseudo-Cicero, *Ad Herennium* III §35.

And so the rule of thumb for developing Pictures for one's Memory Palace might be summarized as *the stranger the better*: experiences and encounters that are novel tend to stay in the memory, while those that are commonplace are quickly forgotten.[32] As Frankt puts it, "The best memorizers place the most flamboyant, bizarre, crude and lewd images and scenes (and their actions) in their memory palaces. The more distinctive, the more easily they're recalled."[33]

The Memory Palace in practice

So what did this look like in practice? In a later chapter we will walk through the process for today's preachers crafting their sermons and learning them by heart using the canons of rhetoric and the Memory Palace, in particular. Let us take just a moment here, though, and listen to Quintilian's approach for applying this classical method in classical times.

He starts by remarking on the power of *place*. "When we return to a certain place after an interval," he writes, "we not only recognize it but remember what we did there, persons are recalled, and sometimes even unspoken thoughts come back to mind."[34] Then he turns to giving practical advice on selecting Places for their Memory Palace. "Students learn Places (*loci*) which are as extensive as possible and are marked by a variety of objects, perhaps a large house divided into many separate areas." Along these lines, he also invokes Cicero: "The Places we adopt should be numerous, well lit, clearly defined, and at moderate intervals."[35] Most impor-

32. In this way your Pictures provide a contrast to your Place. The latter you want to be pedestrian; unhelpful (and frankly terrifying) would be the house whose rooms are constantly shuffling location. The former you want to be remarkable and extraordinary, so as to stand out in the mind.

33. Frakt, "An Ancient and Proven Way."

34. Quintilian, *Instituto Oratoria* 11.2 §17. He adds, "So, as usual, Art was born of Experience."

35. Quintilian, *Instituto Oratoria* 11.2 §22. Cf. Cicero, *De Oratore* 2.358. Quintilian further notes, "What I said about a house can be done also with public buildings, a long road, a town perambulation, or pictures. One can even

tant, though, is that the Place be utterly familiar: "The first task is to make sure that it all comes to mind without any hold-up, because a memory which is to help another memory has to be something more than secure."[36] You cannot anchor on a moving object.

Having secured the Place, Quintilian turns to the Pictures— "the aids we use to mark what we have to learn by heart." Thus, in developing one's Memory Palace, "The next stage is to mark what they have written or are mentally preparing with some sign which will jog their memory."[37] Interestingly, he comments in passing on why this system works: "Pictures are very effective, and one memory leads to another—just as a ring put on a different finger or tied with a thread reminds us why we did these things. These Pictures acquire even more binding force when people transfer memory from some similar object to the item which has to be remembered."[38] And once again he will call on old Tullius: "The Images [should be] effective, sharp, distinctive, and such as can come to mind and make a quick impression."[39] When in doubt, listen to Cicero.

Now the orator puts the pieces together, imagining a speech on naval warfare. "Let us suppose a symbol of navigation, such as an anchor, or of warfare, such as a weapon," he writes, narrating the process of classical orators. "They place the first idea, as it were, in the vestibule, the second, let us say, in the atrium, and then they go round the open areas, assigning ideas systematically not only to bedrooms and bays, but to statues and the like." Then it's a matter of retracing one's mnemonic steps. Yates comments, "We have to think of the ancient orator as moving in imagination through his

invent these settings for oneself."

36. Quintilian, *Institutio Oratoria* 11.2 §18.

37. Quintilian, *Institutio Oratoria* 11.2 §18.

38. Quintilian, *Institutio Oratoria* 11.2 §30.

39. Cicero, *De Oratore* 2.358. One possible misunderstanding to address. It is not (necessarily) the case that the Picture in one's Memory Palace is actually part of the speech; in fact, more often than not it is not. The Ad Herennium's lawyer is not going to talk about ram's testicles; she's going to talk about witnesses. The purpose of the Picture is simply to facilitate recall. Much more on this anon.

memory building *whilst* he is making his speech, drawing from the memorized places the images he has placed on them."[40] Quintilian thus continues:

> This done, when they have to revive the memory, they begin to go over these Places from the beginning, calling in whatever they deposited with each of them, as the images remind them. Thus, however many things have to be remembered, they become a single item, held together as it were by a sort of outer shell, so that speakers do not make mistakes by trying to connect what follows with what goes before by the sole effort of learning by heart.

Here, then, is the crux of the Memory Palace: orators associate their ideas and arguments with concrete people and pictures, which can then be arranged throughout a familiar place. So the *Ad Herennum* summarizes: "In like fashion we shall set the other counts of the charge in backgrounds successively, following their order, and whenever we wish to remember a point, by properly arranging the patterns of the backgrounds and carefully imprinting the images, we shall easily succeed in calling back to mind what we wish."[41] The beauty of the method of loci is indeed in its simplicity. By tapping into fundamental human capacities (spatial association, thinking in images) the Memory Palace accelerates and augments the ability of the orator to speak by heart—or the pastor to *preach* by heart.

Concluding caveat

As we conclude this chapter, which has extolled the powers and potential of this classical technique, it would be good to offer a caveat—one already made by the ancients, and no less relevant today. And the caveat is simply this: orators still need to practice.

40. Yates, *Art of Memory,* 18. She also remarks, "The rules summon up a vision of a forgotten social habit. Who is that man moving slowly in the lonely building, stopping at intervals with an intent face? He is a rhetoric student forming a set of memory loci" (24).

41. Pseudo-Cicero, *Ad Herennium* III §34.

So the author of the *Ad Herennium* will wrap up his *tour de force* teaching on the Memory Palace by advising that "in every discipline artistic theory is of little avail without unremitting exercise, but especially in mnemonics theory is almost valueless unless made good by industry, devotion, toil, and care.[42] Quintilian is even more adamant: "If I am asked what is the one great art of Memory, the answer is 'practice and effort': the most important thing is to learn a lot by heart and think a lot out without writing, if possible every day. No other faculty is so much developed by practice or so much impaired by neglect."[43]

The art of memory can help preachers take tremendous strides in their ability to preach without notes. It can facilitate a capacity for preaching by heart that all too many pastors thought impossible. But at the end of the day, it doesn't obviate the need for devoted attention to the craft of public speaking. To be sure, this is not the "drill and kill" method disavowed in the Introduction; as we shall in Part 2, the *nature* of this practice is quite different. Nevertheless, orators of every age have recognized that, inasmuch as public speaking is a skill (and a difficult one at that), it can only be honed through constant training. There is, after all, hardly a more emblematic statement of classical thought than the dictum *usus est magister optimus*: practice is the greatest teacher.

---

42. Pseudo-Cicero, *Ad Herennium* III §40.

43. Quintilian, *Institutio Oratoria* 11.2 §40.

Memory Palace Recap

- Memory (*Memoria*) is the process of learning your speech by heart so that you can deliver it without the use of notes
- Two aspects to memory
    1. Natural memory—innate gifts of remembering
    2. Artificial memory—cultivated skill of remembering
- The Memory Palace (or method of loci) is a mnemonic system of Places (*loci*) and Pictures (*imagines*)
- Rule of thumb: the stranger the better
- The Memory Palace does not negate the need for practice and effort

PART 2:

Contemporary Preaching
and the Memory Palace

Chapter 3

APPLYING CLASSICAL RHETORIC TO SERMON PREPARATION

Introduction

WE NOW TURN TOWARD the practical application of the insights and implications of classical rhetoric generally and the Memory Palace in particular. In the next chapter we will look more specifically at integrating the techniques of the Memory Palace into our practice of preaching by heart. In this chapter, though, we endeavor to approach the process of preparing to preach with fresh eyes, coming at it from the question: how does (or should) *sermon delivery* affect *preaching preparation?*

That this question is essential to the homiletic task would seem to be obvious, and yet is all too often overlooked or disregarded—as though the actual sermon delivery were incidental to preaching! Toward the end of his excellent homiletics textbook *The Witness of Preaching*, Thomas Long makes this point:

> In earlier chapters we explored the crucial steps a preacher takes in moving toward a sermon: interpreting a biblical text, creating a form, deciding about the use of illustrative material, and so on. Even though these activities have traditionally been thought of as 'preparing the sermon,' it would be more accurate, given the

orality of preaching, to describe these steps as preparing for the sermon. Since most of these preliminary activities have involved reading and writing, one final step must be taken as we go from the desk to the pulpit: the move from writing to speaking.[1]

Along similar lines, Joseph Webb observes that if the preacher's goal is to preach without notes then that must transform how one approaches the whole preaching task. He writes, "The decision to preach a sermon without notes should be made before the sermon is prepared, not after. This is because preaching without notes requires one to prepare in some strikingly different ways than if one plans to write out and preach from a manuscript, or even to preach from an extensively worked outline."[2] In other words, if the pastor intends to preach by heart on Sunday, then she needs to change how she approaches preparing to preach starting on Monday.

As we saw in Part I, *Memoria* is part of the so-called "canons of rhetoric." These canons were not mere theoretical constructs or analytical tools; they were developed by practicing orators in antiquity for the purpose of preparing speeches. While they may still receive passing attention in a public speaking or homiletics class, they are not being given their full due—especially for preachers. So in this chapter we will draw on our previous discussion of the canons in chapter 1 to sketch out a weekly process for pastors to prepare *for* preaching (as Tom Long would remind us)[3] that privileges sermon delivery.

1. Long, *The Witness of Preaching*, 263 (emphasis my own).

2. Webb, *Preaching without Notes*, 35.

3. Pastors have varying "work weeks," with some only getting one day off a week and others two; some taking Mondays off, some Fridays, etc. For simplicity's sake, and recognizing of course that pastors are always "on call," I am assuming a pastor who is in the office four days a week, plus the Lord's Day. See also Paul Scott Wilson's structure in *The Practice of Preaching*.

Day 1: *Inventio* (Discovery)

The place where there may be the most overlap between the classical approach to developing an oration and the modern practice of sermon development is probably in this first canon, *Inventio*—the process of Discovery. The reason that this canon continues to have such contemporary resonance is the universal recognition that before you can say *something* you have to have something *to say.* Preparation starts with investigation: seeking out the sources and substance of the message. This is the task of *Inventio.*

Let's consider what this day and stage commonly looks like for pastors. It's the first day of the "work week," so to speak. Pastors may make this the very first part of their first day—before answering emails, before putting out fires from the weekend, before making visits (unless there's an emergency)—because they recognize that it is, in Steven Covey's metaphor, a "big rock."[4] They want to get to it before other things clutter up the day. And so the pastor sits down at his desk and surrounds himself with books: in addition to the Bible, there are a multitude of commentaries, volumes from the *Theological Dictionary of the New Testament*, collections of sermons, and so on. This being the twenty-first century, the pastor may also be using electronic resources like Logos or Accordance. In whatever format such resources come in, in this *Inventio* stage the preacher is like a magnet attracting pertinent material from all these various and sundry sources.

Pastors of course develop their own personal routines for this *Inventio* stage of sermon preparation. What follows is one possible approach, recognizing that each preacher's manner and mileage will vary.[5] The reader might think of the panoply of resources like concentric circles, rippling out from the *font* of Scripture. The first circle is within Scripture itself: context, parallel passages, cross

4. The picture is a jar that is being filled with three elements: big rocks, gravel, and sand. They correspond, respectively, to your most important responsibilities, necessary tasks, and trivial matters. See Covey, *First Things First*, chapter 4.

5. See also, e.g., Wilson, *Practice of Preaching*, 1–54; Long, *Witness of Preaching*, 76–112.

references, and so on. If the preacher is in a church that uses the lectionary, this will also include the other assigned texts for the Sunday. This exegetical discipline is an instantiation of the hermeneutical principle of Scripture interpreting Scripture; before we hear what others have had to say about the text, we listen to the witness of the canonical authors—and so the divine Author.

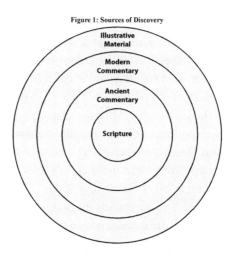

Figure 1: Sources of Discovery

The second circle comprises ancient and pre-modern interpreters of the text, especially patristic authors.[6] This circle is important for at least three reasons. First, this early commentary is illuminating for discerning the reception history of the Scripture, especially when it comes to controverted passages. Turning to this second circle of interpreters is sort of like being among a group of friends that, encountering some surprise, look at each other as if to say, "Are you hearing what I'm hearing?" Second, being closer historically and culturally to the *Sitz im Leben* of the Bible, these authors may help to fill in interpretive "blanks" in the text: they can help to explain or make sense of things that are distant or foreign to our ears.[7] And third, as a matter of particular importance for

6. A very helpful resource for this second "circle" is the Ancient Christian Commentary on Scripture series, edited by the late Thomas Oden and published by InterVarsity Press.

7. On "blanks" in the text, see Voelz, *What Does This Mean?*, chapters 7–8.

preachers, this circle of interpreters is relentlessly *christocentric*. As R. R. Reno and John O'Keefe put it in their book on early Christian interpretation of the Bible, "Jesus Christ is the crucial, recapitulating figure, and for that reason he discloses the logic of the divine economy and functions as the hub of interpretation around which the other figures revolve. Indeed, insofar as the church fathers treat interpretation of the scriptural texts as the privileged means for understanding all of reality, Jesus Christ functions as the hub of all reality."[8] Attending to the second circle keeps Christ at the center.

The third circle is modern commentary on the Scripture. Placing such commentary in this tertiary position is not to degrade its importance—indeed, in many cases the exegesis is superior to that of pre-moderns—but to recognize that being a Christian and a pastor is to be part of a great tradition that reaches back further than fifty or even five hundred years. Hearing those more ancient voices first keeps the contemporary ones in proper perspective, ensuring that theological and pastoral concerns—ever present in pre-modern Christian commentary—are not crowded out by the technical and critical concerns that tend to predominate in contemporary commentaries.[9] Both are important, and both need their proper place.

A final circle in the *Inventio* preparation consists of any resources that might not fall under traditional biblical commentary but that can still be pertinent to the preaching task, particularly in gleaning illustrative material. This may include a short story from Flannery O'Connor, an article in the *Wall Street Journal*, or a Facebook post from a friend. As preachers well know, these unorthodox (which is not to say heretical) sources can provide inspiration and a different slant on familiar topics.

So, then, in the *Inventio* stage preachers are collecting sources and insights like a lawyer collecting evidence. At this point the goal is simply to establish the basic meaning of the text(s), and what general direction to take the sermon. The final product of this

---

8. O'Keefe and Reno, *Sanctified Vision*, 81.

9. A marvelous exception to this rule is the excellent *Brazos Theological Commentary on the Bible*.

process will be something like the simple pair of statements that Thomas Long calls the "focus and function":[10] a *focus* statement that sets out the central theme (e.g., "How Christ reconciles people to God and to one another"), and a *function* statement that sets out the goal of the sermon (e.g., "That the hearers might pursue forgiveness and reconciliation within the body of Christ"). Now, the preacher is ready to move to Day 2 and the canon of *Dispositio*.[11]

Day 1 (Discovery) Recap

- *Discovery* is seeking out the sources and substance of the sermon
- Gather the raw material for the message
    - Scripture first and foremost, then other sources:
        - (1) Ancient commentary
        - (2) Modern commentary
        - (3) Illustrative material
        - (4) Other
- Generate a focus or theme

Day 2: *Dispositio* (Arrangement)

In a 2013 essay for *The New Yorker*, legendary journalist John McPhee describes a scenario that is all too familiar for the preacher: "I had done all the research I was going to do, assembled enough material to fill a silo. And now I had no idea what to do with it." That was early in his career. What changed everything for him, though, was discovering a humble hero: Structure. McPhee writes, "A compelling structure in nonfiction can have an attracting effect analogous to a story line in fiction." He goes on:

---

10. Long, *Witness of Preaching*, chapter 4.

11. While this process will of course vary from preacher to preacher (and circumstance to circumstance), for myself I generally allot three to four hours on Monday for *Inventio* work.

> The approach to structure in factual writing is like re-
> turning from a grocery store with materials you intend
> to cook for dinner. You set them out on the kitchen
> counter, and what's there is what you deal with, and all
> you deal with. If something is red and globular, you don't
> call it a tomato if it's a bell pepper. To some extent, the
> structure of a composition dictates itself, and to some
> extent it does not. Where you have a free hand, you can
> make interesting choices.[12]

McPhee is writing about journalism and not preaching, but
his comments are still apt: *structure matters*. While the focus of this
book is principally *Memoria* and the Memory Palace, one is tempted to assert that *Dispositio*—Structure, or Arrangement—is in fact
the most overlooked and underutilized of the canons in sermon
preparation. Arrangement, the reader will recall, is the purposeful structuring of ideas and experiences in the speech or sermon;
or, as Plato had it, Arrangement is the well-butchered bird. This
canon is oft overlooked because preachers, being human, easily fall
into familiar paths and patterns of proclamation. We tend to find
a structure that works and stick with it. In my Lutheran tradition
the default is a kind of law-then-gospel structure, summarized by
a confirmand thusly: "You're bad. Jesus is good. Amen."[13]

On the one hand, there's nothing inherently wrong with this.
The word of God, which does the work of converting and sanc-
tifying, can still be proclaimed. And if the people of God know
what to expect, that can even aid their comprehension: they know
where things are going and can follow the steps like a well-worn
path. But this is also, on the other hand, the problem: if the assem-
bly knows where the preacher is going they may well tune out, the
way someone can drive to their workplace without thinking about
it.[14] Moreover, preachers themselves may become bored with proc-

12. McPhee, "Structure."

13. For a critique of this approach, see Schmitt, "Richard Caemmerer's
Goal, Malady, Means."

14. I note in passing that this phenomenon is further evidence for the value
of spatial memory and the Places (*loci*) component of the Memory Palace
technique.

lamation, serving up a warmed-over boilerplate that excites them no more than their hearers.

Arrangement can help to address drab preaching, while also facilitating *Memoria*. By introducing varying structures into the proclamation, a single message can be preached in a variety of ways. Think of poetry. With its manifold structures and forms, poetry is able to explore the same topic from many different angles. One can speak of love, for example, in the exalted form of a Shakespearean sonnet, or in the playful form of a limerick. A preacher who only uses a single structure (even unintentionally so) becomes like a poet who composes only couplets.

Additionally, Arrangement helps to facilitate *Memoria* by providing a clear structure. To use the poetry analogy once again, memorizing a poem in free verse versus one in iambic pentameter is significantly more difficult. The outcome is obvious. Since the preacher's sermon structure is mapped on to the structure of the Memory Palace, arranging discrete moments and movements— like a house that flows well from room to room—is key. Open floor plans might be all the rage in contemporary architecture, but they're no help for the Memory Palace.

So, then, how does one practice Arrangement, intentionally integrating a variety of structures into the sermon preparation?[15] Consider an exercise inspired by Daniel Overdorf in his book *One Year to Better Preaching*, which we will call the One-Sentence Sermon exercise.[16] It works like this. As noted above, the fruit of *Inventio* is the focus or theme statement. The preacher then takes that statement and distills it to a single word or phrase; for the illustration mentioned above, that word might be "reconciliation." Then, he runs that concept through a host of textual, thematic, and dynamic structures.[17] For each, he writes out a "one-sentence

15. For more on integrating sermon structures in sermon preparation, see, e.g., Buttrick, *Homiletic Moves and Structures*, Part II, and Arthurs, *Preaching with Variety*.

16. Overdorf, *One Year to Better Preaching*, 159–66.

17. For some ideas for different structures I recommend Arthur's *Preaching With Variety*, Aristotle's *Ars Rhetorica* (especially Book II), and a website produced by David Schmitt and hosted by Concordia Seminary: www.

sermon" that employs that structure and points up how the theme might be developed using it.[18] Let's look at our example of reconciliation using a few different structures:

Figure 2: One-Sentence Sermons

One-Sentence sermons: Reconciliation

- Analogy (thematic): Reconciliation is like the process of creating a truce between warring parties.

- Compare/contrast (thematic): Christian reconciliation contrasts from worldly reconciliation in its source, depth, and aims.

- Verse-by-Verse (textual): In 2 Corinthians 5, Saint Paul sets out the motive for reconciliation (vv. 14-15), the message of reconciliation (vv. 16-19), and the ministers of reconciliation (vv. 20-21).

- Homiletical plot (dynamic): If Jesus came to effect reconciliation, why does He say that He did not come to bring peace but a sword?

In each of these instances, one can imagine—if only in an inchoate way—how the sermon might be arranged using that structure. To be sure, some texts and themes better lend themselves to some structures (or class of structures) than others. The goal for the exercise is simply to break out of the rut of using the same structure over and over, and indeed to challenge oneself to employ different structures and so see a particular text in a different way.[19] The poet W. H. Auden used to boast that he had (or could) compose a poem in any form known to humanity. Preachers would do well to have such ambition with the Arrangement of their sermons. Their hearers will certainly appreciate the effort.

---

concordiatheology.com/pulpit.

18. These "sermons" needn't be exactly one sentence; the idea is that the theme be very briefly sketched in a way that suggests how it could be further developed using that particular structure.

19. As the pastor of a church that uses the lectionary, I find this especially rewarding. One year I may preach on a pericope using a thematic structure, while the next time it comes up I use a dynamic one. In this way, the lectionary's appointed texts continue to stay fresh—and, Lord willing, so does the preaching.

Day 2 (Arrangement) Recap

- *Arrangement* is the purposeful structuring of ideas and experiences in the sermon
- Complete the One-Sentence Sermon exercise
- Determine what structure best suits the message

Day 3: *Elocutio* (Style)

By now it is midweek and the preacher has settled on a theme that is the product of significant study and reflection (*Inventio*) and plotted out the development of this theme using a particular structure (*Dispositio*). This next stage, or canon, is the crossroads of preparing for the sermon. Cicero, as cited in chapter 2, defines *Elocutio* as "the fitting of the proper language to the invented matter.[20]" Most just call it Style. This is the stage at which preachers will do most of their actual composition, in whatever form that may take (I'll make my own suggestion presently).

Style is a sticky wicket for preachers. Some (pretend to) eschew it altogether, forgetting that even "plain" is its own style.[21] Others might grow too enamored with Style and find themselves lost in the weeds of wordsmithing. Neither approach is all that helpful. I would instead like to advocate an approach to Style that is suggested by the ancients, then focus in on one element of Style that is particularly pertinent to the preaching task—and even more so for those who aspire to preach by heart.

Sketching the sermon

First, for establishing our general approach to Style in preaching preparation, we return to our good friend Quintilian. Addressing

---

20. Cicero, *De Inventione* I.VII §9.

21. The plain style is most closely associated with the American Puritans. See, e.g., Houser, "Puritan Homiletics."

those who have either insufficient powers of natural memory[22] (some preachers) or insufficient time with which to learn their material by heart (most every preacher), he writes, "It will be useless to tie yourself down to every word, since forgetting just one word will bring on shameful hesitation or even reduce you to silence. It is much safer to get a good grasp of the bare facts and then leave yourself freedom in expressing them."[23] In short: when it comes to Style, it's just the facts, ma'am.

This recognition of the necessity of those "bare facts" has inspired an approach to Style that I have come to call *sketching the sermon*. When sketching the sermon, it is helpful to think like a journalist.[24] With each movement, or section, of the sermon preachers will want to ask themselves: what's the lead? What is the essential content—the "hook"—upon which the whole of the rhetorical unit can be hung? Rather than rabbit-trailing into the niceties of syntax and sentence structure—important for the written word, less so for public speaking—sketching the sermon ensures that the preacher zeroes in on the core content to be conveyed.[25] From these "bare facts" the remainder of the exposition flows.

Let it be said, though, that sketching the sermon does not mean watering down its substance. The point is not to produce Diet Jesus. On the contrary, sketching the sermon means that instead of getting lost in those things that, while perhaps good and interesting, distract from the core message, preachers put their time, energy, and creativity into developing the essential substance of the sermon. The sketch of a house plan may not include every electrical outlet, but it will show the most important things: the form of architecture, the flow of the floor plan, the shape of the

22. Recall from chapter 2 that "natural" memory is the inborn capacity for remembering, as contrasted with "artificial" memory, which is the cultivated skill for remembering.

23. Quintilian, *Institutio Oratoria* 11.2 §49.

24. See Heath and Heath, *Made to Stick*, 75–76.

25. This has the added benefit of helping the preacher to resist the temptation of creating a sermon that is too *precious*, with words painstakingly applied like paint to a decorative egg. Smash the egg; embrace the sketch.

rooms. So also the sermon sketch ensures that we don't miss the building for the beams.

What, then, does the sermon sketch look like? Some, especially at first, will still compose something close to an abridged manuscript. For most—and this is where I have landed—it will look something like an inchoate outline: bullet points with catch-phrases, sentence fragments, and story lines that occupy the movements of the sermon. The goal is not to have each thought fully fleshed out, but to set out in abbreviated fashion the handful of ideas, images, arguments, etc., that the preacher wishes to impart in each section.[26] And this brings us to the element of Style that is most helpful in preparing to preach by heart.

The Universal Language

In their book *Made to Stick,* Chip and Dan Heath recount the story of a firm that produced the complicated machinery used to make silicon chips. The company relied on two groups of people: engineers to create the design, and manufacturers to construct the design. Alas, the two groups spoke different languages, with the engineers caught up in the clouds of abstraction and the manufacturers thinking about the tactile realities of the machines themselves. Ultimately, the engineers needed to change their behavior and communicate at the level of the physical machine—since that was a "language" shared by everyone. The Heaths conclude, "The moral of this story is not to 'dumb things down.' The manufacturing people faced complex problems and they needed smart answers. Rather, the moral of the story is to find a 'universal language,' one that everyone speaks fluently. *Inevitably, that universal language will be concrete.*"[27]

The same could be said of preachers. Preachers are the engineers, so to speak, of this firm called church. They have the high-falutin' knowledge, if not the beatific vision. In order to convey

---

26. For an example of the sermon sketch, see the sermon exhibit in the Conclusion.

27. Heath and Heath, *Made to Stick,* 115; emphasis my own.

that adequately to the people of God—the ones caught up in the physical, tangible realities of living by faith in the everyday and mundane—preachers need to speak in the universal language of analogy, metaphor, and story. It is cliché by now to point out, as St. Matthew did, that "all these [teachings] Jesus said to the crowds in parables; indeed, he said nothing to them without a parable" (Matt 13:34). And yet the observation being commonplace does not render it any less true—and perhaps pastors might do well to take it more deeply to heart. The Lord was the master of the concrete word. And in proclaiming the gospel by saying "the kingdom of heaven is like . . ." Jesus spoke not only a universal *message*, but a universal *language*.

Happily, the Memory Palace both requires and rewards such language. As we have seen, it promotes creativity in developing Pictures to encapsulate the content of the sermon. It goes further than that, however. Wearisome would be the task for the preacher who constantly found herself needing to translate abstract ideas into Pictures for her Memory Palace. Much more effective—and, we might add, more enjoyable—is to be incorporating concrete language and images into the sermon itself. Instead of resorting to theological ideas or (worse still) abstruse jargon, the pastor who aspires to preach by heart effectively will find analogies and anecdotes that keep the sermon rooted in everyday realities.

Concrete elements not only lend themselves more easily to association with Pictures for the Memory Palace, but also are more memorable. The British classicist Eric Havelock spent a lifetime studying stories that were passed down orally, particularly the epics of Homer. In his *Preface to Plato*, he observes how such tales are remarkable for their preponderance of concrete details.[28] "When they were passed along from generation to generation, the more memorable concrete details survived and the abstractions evaporated."[29] To be sure, these concrete elements can—and often do—overlap with the "lead" of the sermon, mentioned above.

---

28. Havelock, *Preface to Plato*.
29. Heath and Heath, *Made to Stick*, 107.

Taken together with the "5 Ws,"[30] this makes for an effective way to sketch the sermon with Style.

Day 3 (Style) Recap

- Style is "the fitting of the proper language to the invented matter" (Cicero)
  - Principal stage of composition
- "Sketch" the sermon by setting out its essential content in rough outline fashion
- Focus on the concrete elements of story, metaphor, etc.

Interlude

We have rounded the corner on the preacher's week and the substance of the sermon is now in place. With the Memory Palace in view and preaching by heart as our aim, the first three days have moved us toward preparing *for* the sermon and not merely in readying a document to be read. With the next stage—the *Memoria* day, as it were—we will turn to the construction of the Memory Palace. Then, finally, we will discuss how the proclamation on Sunday morning plays out, and the pulpit is transformed into the Palace. This is the burden of our next chapter.

---

30. Who, what, where, when, and why.

Chapter 4

CONSTRUCTING THE MEMORY PALACE

Introduction

THE RAW MATERIALS FOR constructing our Memory Palace have been gathered (*Inventio*). The blueprint's been established, the walls and rooms have been framed (*Dispostio*). The decor has been provided and the furnishings fabricated (*Elocutio*). Now the time has come to identify the Place for our Palace and to create the dynamic Pictures that will populate it. These two steps are the work of *Memoria* proper, where the method of loci takes full effect. Then, finally, we will have arrived at Sunday be ready to "occupy" the Palace, inviting the people of God to dwell in the proclaimed Word: this is the actual Delivery of the sermon (*Pronuntiatio*). To these latter two stages we now turn.

Day 4: Memoria (Memory)

At its essence, as we have said, the method of loci is a mnemonic system of Places and Pictures, sites and symbols. We thus have two tasks to undertake at this stage: 1) to pick a Place that we wish to use as the backdrop for our Memory Palace, and 2) to "paint" the potent Pictures that will point up the content of the sermon.

Step 1: Picking a Place for your Palace

Recall the operative principle for the Memory Palace, which we discussed in chapter 2. In one memory master's words, it is "to use one's exquisite spatial memory to structure and store information whose order comes less naturally."[1] It is at this point where that becomes most apparent: the practical task of selecting a *locus*, a Place, for your Memory Palace. What location should you use? And do you need more than one? To begin here we turn to a sixteenth-century Jesuit missionary.

Three kinds of Places

Matteo Ricci wanted to bring the gospel to the Chinese. Ricci had received the customary classical education for Jesuits of his time, which included training in rhetoric generally and the art of memory in particular. As a method to endear himself to his Asian hosts, in 1596 Ricci taught them the secrets of the Memory Palace. His practical advice to the Chinese, recounted in Jonathan Spence's book *The Memory Palace of Matteo Ricci,* is still helpful for us today.[2] Ricci suggested that there were three main options for selecting "memory locations." First, he said, they could come from reality itself. By this, he meant from buildings or objects that a person was already acquainted with. Second, Ricci says that your location could be imaginary: a place that you conjure in your mind, of any shape and size. Or third, he says, it could be a combination thereof: part real and part imaginary. For example, he says, "as in the case of a building one knew well and through the back wall of which one broke an imaginary door as a shortcut to new spaces."[3]

---

1. Foer, *Moonwalking with Einstein,* 98.
2. Spence, *The Memory Palace of Matteo Ricci.*
3. Spence, *The Memory Palace of Matteo Ricci,* 1–2.

Kinds of Places (*loci*)

1. Real Places
2. Imaginary Places
3. Hybrid (Real/Imaginary) Places

Let's ponder each of Ricci's suggested options. The first and most natural source of your *locus* is a real place that you know well. Close your eyes for a moment. Recall such a spot; say, your childhood home. Now, take a walk in your mind through that place. Do you get lost? Probably not. There's the foyer, say. Then you take a left turn and find yourself in the living room. It connects to a den in the back. You come out of there into a hallway. And so on. The pathways of places we know well are etched in our memories, like the route of Eugene Pauly's neighborhood walk.

Real places—and places you know *really well*—are still the gold standard for the Memory Palace. The reason is simply that you do not want to be thinking about your Places, but your Pictures; your location needs to be somewhere that you can pass through effortlessly, in order that your mind may be fixed on the furnishings. "The first task is to make sure that it all comes to mind without any hold-up," Quintilian wrote, "because a memory which is to help another memory has to be something more than secure."[4] And so good candidates for your *locus*, in addition to those already mentioned, include your church, the campus of your alma mater, or a neighborhood park. Whether it's inside or outside, geometric or irregular, large or small—these considerations are all subservient to the one main criterion of familiarity.

But what if, for whatever reason, the places you know well simply aren't lending themselves well to the construction of your Memory Palace? Or what if (as Matteo Ricci more had in view) you want many *loci* so as to expand your mind-storage? We'll return presently to the question of how many such palaces preachers need, but for the moment let's entertain Ricci's second suggested

---

4. Quintilian, *Institutio Oratoria* 11.2 §19.

option for a memory location: the imagination. Already 400 years ago Ricci anticipated what modern researchers have discovered, namely, that even fabricated memory locations can be remarkably effective for serial recall. A 2012 study at the University of Alberta had participants use a briefly studied virtual *locus* as the basis for their Memory Palace, and then apply the strategy to several lists of unrelated words. According to the researchers, "When our virtual environments were used, the MOL (method of loci) was as effective, compared to an uninstructed control group, as the traditional MOL where highly familiar environments were used."[5] The bottom line is that an imaginary (or "virtual") Memory Palace may be nearly as effective as a real one.[6]

The third option that Ricci suggested was a "hybrid" Memory Palace: a real location augmented with imaginary details—your house, for instance, but with a fabricated sun room off the back. What would be the benefit of this arrangement? Consider an analogous situation. A family recognizes that their home is not sufficient to meet their growing needs. They love their house, however; it has the lived-in familiarity of a pair of well-worn jeans. And so rather than sell and relocate, they opt to add on. A similar phenomenon can happen when it comes to the Memory Palace. A preacher finds himself expanding his homiletical reach—either with a longer sermon, or more complex one—and rather than start afresh with a novel *locus*, he opts to add on. Then, instead of learning an all-new Memory Palace in addition to the content it "houses," he will only need to familiarize himself with a new room or two. The comfort of his memory-home is still intact.

The main point when it comes to selecting a location for your Memory Palace, for sources both ancient and modern, is that you must you must know your location very well; if you need to think too hard about it, then that defeats the whole purpose. As Joshua

---

5. Legge et al., "Building a memory palace in minutes."

6. Note, however, that the researchers in the University of Alberta study were not using the method of loci for the purpose of oratory but simply for memory recall.

Foer puts it, "the crucial thing" for the Memory Palace is that a location be "intimately familiar."[7]

How many Places do you need?

But this raises the question, alluded to above, about *how many* Memory Palaces a preacher needs. This is all a matter of aims. If one is utilizing the method of loci in order to retain vast stores of information, such as a medical student memorizing numerous diseases and disorders, then a whole "memory neighborhood" may be needed. If you are Giordano Bruno, seeking to keep the whole sum of human knowledge, you need to erect a ginormous memory stadium.[8] If, however, you are a preacher whose aim in using the Memory Palace is more in keeping with its original purpose—to facilitate preaching by heart—you may need only a handful of *loci*, or even just one.

Someone who is called upon to speak at a variety of churches and venues may want to have several messages committed to memory, in which case it might be helpful to have multiple *loci* to keep them all in order. This is not the experience of the typical parish pastor, however. It is fair to say that most preachers need to be able to preach by heart only the next Sunday's sermon—and, if it's Lent or Advent, an additional midweek or festival service. In this case, the preacher may only need one Place, which can be "cleaned out" after each Lord's Day service.[9] But that brings us to Step 2 and the Pictures of your Memory Palace.

---

7. Foer, *Moonwalking with Einstein*, 98.

8. See Yates, *The Art of Memory*.

9. The classical writers were conspicuously quiet about how to reuse their palaces; perhaps they regarded it as sufficiently straightforward that they needn't comment on it.

Step 2: Painting Potent Pictures

How does a melange of biblical quotations, anecdotes, arguments, and analogies become a memorable message? What kind of alchemy is necessary to turn the furnishings of your Memory Palace into unforgettable features? This is the next step in the method of loci, which I dub *painting potent Pictures*.[10] In technical terms, it is known as *elaborative encoding*: "the formation of associative connections with other memory traces . . . [which] occurs most effectively where meaningful associations can be found."[11] Ed Cooke describes it more colorfully: "The general idea . . . is to change whatever boring thing is being inputted into your memory into something that is so colorful, so exciting, and so different from anything you've seen before that you can't possibly forget it . . . That's what elaborate encoding is.[12]" Elaborative encoding gets at what Pseudo-Cicero was talking about two millennia prior when he adumbrated the *imagines agentes*, the "active images." As he put it, "Ordinary things easily slip from the memory while the striking and novel stay longer in mind."[13] Thus the key, according to Cooke, is to convert what one wants to remember (such as the content of a sermon) into compelling images: "By laying down elaborate, engaging, vivid images in your mind, it more or less guarantees that your brain is going to end up storing a robust, dependable memory."[14] Such images are more naturally etched in the mind.

How, then, is this "elaborative encoding"—this painting potent Pictures—done? Three principal strategies from the tradition stand out, which I shall term Association, Exaggeration, and Similarity. And in order to see how these strategies can work in practice, we will do some "reverse engineering," so to speak, of a few sermon selections. That is, we will analyze and imagine how, were

10. "Potent" in order to keep in mind that, as we mentioned earlier, these are not static images but dynamic ones.

11. Groome, *An Introduction to Cognitive Psychology*, 168. See also Brown and Craik, "Encoding and Retrieval of Information."

12. Foer, *Moonwalking with Einstein*, 91.

13. Pseudo-Cicero, *Rhetorica ad Herennium* III §35.

14. Foer, *Moonwalking with Einstein*, 99.

one to be preparing to deliver this particular message, the method of loci process might develop. For the sake of simplicity, and also due to his own association with the Memory Palace, we will use sermons from that noted orator and homiletician, St. Augustine.[15]

And speaking of simplicity's sake, before we continue one caveat about Pictures is in order. Despite the technical term of "elaborative encoding," the Pictures should not be thought of as code to be deciphered. They are more like creative mnemonic devices. Their purpose is not to conceal the sermon's content but to encapsulate it in memorable images. The Pictures prompt the preacher's recollection of the message through pictorial means, like how leafing through a family photo album prompts memories of the moments and events that they depict. The reader is encouraged to keep this caveat in mind if what follows seems unduly complex. Its final destination is simplicity, but it is (to paraphrase Oliver Wendell Holmes) the simplicity on the far side of complexity.

Strategies for Painting Potent Pictures

1. Association—*think like Zooey*

2. Exaggeration—*think like Marco*

3. Similarity—*think like Amelia Bedelia*

Strategy 1: Association

The first strategy is *Association*. To understand how this works we can take inspiration from J. D. Salinger's novel *Franny & Zooey*. In the book, Zooey is an erstwhile child actor, and at one point he recounts to his sister Franny the secret from his youth for managing

---

15. Note that, while Augustine's sermons have of course been transcribed and published, their delivery would typically have been extemporaneous and without notes. See the seminal article by Deferrari, "St. Augustine's Method of Composing and Delivering Sermons." There are an abundance of published volumes of Augustine's sermons, but I will be drawing from the vivid translation by William Griffin in Augustine, *Sermons to the People*.

to stand on stage and unflappably, unfailingly deliver his lines. His brother Seymour had told him to envision "the Fat Lady":

> He never did tell me who the Fat Lady was, but I shined my shoes for the Fat Lady every time I ever went on the air again—all the years you and I were on the program together, if you remember. I don't think I missed more than just a couple of times. This terribly clear, clear picture of the Fat Lady formed in my mind. I had her sitting on this porch all day, swatting flies, with her radio going full-blast from morning till night. I figured the heat was terrible, and she probably had cancer, and—I don't know. Anyway, it seemed goddam clear why Seymour wanted me to shine my shoes when I went on the air. It made sense.[16]

To be sure, Zooey is not practicing a quasi-Memory Palace here. But notice what he does do, which is relevant to our present discussion: he makes a concrete connection by linking a flesh and blood person to his intangible thought or idea.[17] Zooey is demonstrating the strategy of Association. It works like this. The content of the preacher's sermon may *explicitly* reference a particular person (such as St. Paul), or it may *subjectively* call a particular person to the preacher's mind (such as her Aunt Gina). Having associated an element of the sermon with a certain person, like Zooey's Fat Lady, the preacher then plops that person into her Memory Palace.

We see this demonstrated in the *Ad Herennium*. The author gives the example of a prosecutor who desires to remember as part of his case the victim of poisoning. So he writes, "We shall picture the man in question as lying ill in bed, if we know his person. If we do not know him, we shall yet take some one to be our invalid, but not a man of the lowest class, so that he may come to mind at once."[18] It is important to underscore, too, that the logic or rea-

---

16. Salinger, *Franny and Zooey*, 200–201.

17. What he also does, which we will elaborate upon presently, is make his concrete personage especially multisensory. This is a great aid to memory as well.

18. Pseudo-Cicero, *Rhetorica ad Herennium* III §33.

sonableness of this association is irrelevant—and, indeed, from a memory standpoint, the more unreasonable or ridiculous the association, the better.

To imagine how this might work in practice, let's turn to a Christmas sermon from St. Augustine. In this movement of the sermon, Augustine is anticipating objections to the biblical accounts of Jesus' birth. To do so, he develops an imagined dialogue with a pair of heretical opponents whom he dubs "Heckle and Jeckle":

> "Say what you want," the Heretical Hecklers trumpet, "but we know where to find the birth of Christ in the Gospels. And we get the meaning, catch the drift, of the Gospel words. Therefore, we know that the Gospels themselves disagree on the birth of Christ. If Matthew's genealogy's right, then Luke's wrong. Therefore, this disagreement disproves the faith. Therefore, before one can accept the faith, one has to show that there's concord, harmony, in the birth of Christ passages."
>
> "My turn, my dear Heckle and Jeckle. Just how do you demonstrate this so-called discord, disharmony?"
>
> "Well, for us it's a matter of reason and therefore an open and shut case," says Heckle. "But for you it's a matter of faith, which is really rather sad," says Jeckle. "Faith has dulled your hearing so that you can't distinguish one sour note from another."[19]

Augustine has given us plenty of material to work with here. Let's put ourselves in his shoes, imagining for the moment that we were to deliver a sermon that included the ideas in the above rhetorical unit. How might we go about populating this in our Memory Palace? We think of the particular "hecklers" of the faith whom we've encountered and a certain pair come to mind, who for the purposes of the sermon we'll call "Heckle and Jeckle." We picture Jeckle in our Memory Palace, discordantly playing the trumpet into the ears of our neighbor Matthew and our cousin Luke. Meanwhile Heckle is encircling them, opening and shutting a suitcase over and over. From this we are quickly and easily able

19. Augustine, *Sermons to the People*, 12–13.

to recall that the movement is about how opponents to the faith object that Jesus' genealogies in the Gospels of Matthew and Luke lack harmony, and that for them this makes the matter an open-and-shut case.

Understand that I am not suggesting that this is the only approach to developing this content into an image for your Memory Palace—much less that this is how Augustine himself actually did it. The point is that, using the strategy of Association, you populate your Memory Palace with concrete images by associating actual people in your mind with the topics or characters of the sermon. It does not cover every word or sentence in the rhetorical unit; you may end up leaving out the bit about "dulled hearing," or adding more about the heretics' despising faith. The essential substance of the movement is retained, however.

Strategy 2: Exaggeration

The second strategy is *Exaggeration*. To grasp how this way works, consider the classic Dr. Seuss book *And To Think That I Saw It On Mulberry Street*. The narrator is Marco, a young boy who is recounting his journey home from school. His father admonishes him, "Marco, keep your eyelids up and see what you can see." What he can see, it turns out, is more than meets the eye.

"All the long way to school and all the way back," Marco laments, "I've looked and I've looked and I've kept careful track, but all that I've noticed, except my own feet, was a horse and a wagon on Mulberry Street." Unmemorable figures like these simply won't do, as far as Marco is concerned; more drama is needed. "That *can't* be my story," he says. "That's only a *start*. I'll say that a ZEBRA was pulling that cart . . ." Thus the story continues, in delightful Seussian fashion. The zebra soon becomes a reindeer and then an elephant, pulling a chariot that becomes—why, a great big brass band! By the end of the story there's an airplane, the mayor and aldermen, and various and sundry other curious creatures. Marco eagerly heads up his front steps, "For I had a story that no one could beat! And to think that I saw it on Mulberry Street!"[20]

Marco would take naturally to the Memory Palace. His exceptional, outsized imagination accords with what the ancients advised made for the best images and symbols in the method of loci—the strategy of Exaggeration. The *Ad Herennium* author appeals to "nature herself" in teaching this, in a passage already quoted:

> When we see in everyday life things that are petty, ordinary, and banal, we generally fail to remember them, because the mind is not being stirred by anything novel or marvellous. But if we see or hear something exceptionally base, dishonourable, extraordinary, great, unbelievable, or laughable, that we are likely to remember a long time.[21]

The more outrageous and more vivid the image, the better. The strategy of Exaggeration therefore teaches that, when preachers are encoding the content of their sermon into memorable Pictures, they do well to take a page out of Marco's book and turn ho-hum things like wagons and horses into blazing chariots and athletic elephants.

As we have already done, let's work backwards from a passage of one of Augustine's sermons and imagine how the Exaggeration might have operated for the preacher. In a sermon for New Year's Day, Augustine is refuting critics of Christianity (as is his wont) and invokes St. Paul's words to the Romans, "Claiming to be wise, they became fools" (1:22):

> They shouldn't claim for themselves what He'd given them in the first place. Nor should they crow about the stuff He gave them as though they'd earned it themselves. Best thing they could do for themselves would be to admit all this. Then they could hold on to what they saw and be cleansed by Him who'd given them the eyes to see it in the first place. If they'd done this before now, then

20. Dr. Seuss, *And to Think that I Saw it on Mulberry Street*, passim.

21. Pseudo-Cicero, *Rhetorica ad Herennium* III §35.

they could've kept their humility intact, been purged, and emerged to take part in the most blessed contemplation. But of course, sad to say, they didn't.

How could this've happened to them? Well, Pride ran riot. The Liar and the Lionizer came knocking at their souls. They had this preposterous selling proposition. A remarkable new cleanser called Pride that removes the stains from their souls. Side-by-side demonstrations were arranged at purification parties with personal friends of the Demons. This was how the Pagans developed their own rites and liturgies, promising that Pride really could work miracles. As a reward for their pride, they received the anger of God. They should've honored God, but they didn't.[22]

This passage exemplifies how Augustine's colorful, concrete language lends itself well to the Memory Palace generally, and this strategy of Exaggeration specifically. Once again, let us pretend that we were the bishop of Hippo attempting to learn by heart the gist of the above rhetorical unit. How might we proceed? The essence of the first part of this unit is that these critics are too busy touting their own accomplishments to acknowledge the grace of the Creator. In this movement, the verb "crow" is evocative. Correspondingly, what was needed was for the critics' sight to be "cleansed" and so to see creation aright. So here, following the example of our Seussian friend, we might envision a flock of oversized crows, futilely grasping globes in their talons as those eye-cleansing stations—the ones from your high school lab—blast full bore into their faces. Or some such thing.

The second half of this unit is even easier. You imagine a pair of door-to-door salesmen—but not your typical characters. Instead, it's a fearsome lion and the cultural liar *du jour* (if you need help with this one, just turn on the evening news for a bit), and boy do they have a deal for you! They are peddling this miracle cleanser called "Pride"—but it turns out that, when this supposed miracle cleanser is sprayed, the awful anger of God is provoked (say, in the form of lightning bolts from heaven). These

22. Augustine, *Sermons to the People*, 145–46.

exaggerated images, typical of what I have called the strategy of Exaggeration, exemplify another method for converting homiletic content into memorable images. And to think that you saw this in Sunday's sermon!

Strategy 3: Similarity

The third and final method that we will attend to for painting Pictures in one's Memory Palace is the strategy of Similarity. It, too, can be understood from children's literature—this time in the form of the mercurial character of Amelia Bedelia. Amelia is a zealous housekeeper, always eager to fulfill her employers' requests. Unfortunately, she also has a bad habit of either mishearing or misunderstanding (or both) those requests, resulting in ludicrous overly literal fulfillments.

For instance, in *Play Ball, Amelia Bedelia*, due to an unfortunate case of the measles for one of their players the Grizzlies ball club is down a man and so solicits Amelia—who, lo and behold, has never played baseball before—to take his place.[23] Then hilarity ensues. When her teammates urge her to "tag" the baserunner after she picks up a ground ball, Amelia presents a sales tag and pins it to the bewildered ballplayer. When she's alerted that Dick is attempting to "steal" second base, she seizes it and pronounces it safe from any thieves. And when Amelia remarkably launches a deep fly ball, she follows the instruction of her teammates and leaves the field to head home . . . to her house.[24]

The whimsical way of Amelia Bedelia demonstrates the strategy of Similarity. Amelia's way exploits the ambiguity of homophones and homonyms, translating ideas into images by way of similar sounds. This method, typical of classical orators, accounts for the most bizarre detail of the example that we earlier referenced from the *Ad Herennium*. The author is imagining a lawyer attempting to recall that "the defendant killed a man by poison,

23. Parish, *Play Ball, Amelia Bedelia*.

24. To be fair, Amelia Bedelia is neither the first nor the last to be bewildered by the seemingly arbitrary rules and vocabulary of baseball.

has charged that the motive for the crime was an inheritance, and declared that there are many witnesses and accessories to this act."[25] And so he pictures a man laying in bed (the defendant); he is ill and with one hand holding a cup (poisoned), and with the other tablets (the inheritance). But then there's this: "On his fourth finger [are] ram's testicles." Why in the world would that be? Amelia Bedelia is at work here, as it were, because the Latin word for "witnesses," *testis*, sounds similar to *testes*.[26] By making that simple, vivid connection of sounds, the speaker has cemented the image in his memory.

Let's turn once more to a sermon of Augustine to think through this strategy in practice. We will take a selection from an Epiphany sermon. Here, Augustine is introducing the meaning and significance of the feast day:

> Yes, it's a feast day, a festival day, but just what is it we're celebrating? Just what is it I'm supposed to preach about? Well, the feast day is called *Epiphania* in Greek, which in our Latin comes out as *Manifestatio*. Why? This is the day on which the Magi are reported to have paid their respects to the Lord. They were piqued by a star appearing in the sky. Not that they knew it at the time, but the first day they saw it was the day He was born. Somehow they recognized it for what it was. And so from that day to this, they proceeded with all deliberate haste.[27]

Let's consider this like we're playing charades with someone tugging on their ear: "sounds like . . ." Your topic is *Epiphany*, a strange word in its own right that has resonances of both a child making raspberries ("piffff") and "fanny"—thus you might picture a toddler on its fanny sticking its tongue out and blowing bubbles. Is this more than a little ridiculous? Yes, and mnemonists both ancient and modern would remind us that this is why it is effective.

25. Pseudo-Cicero, *Rhetorica ad Herennium* III §33.

26. As to why it's a *ram's* testicles specifically, the translator Harry Caplan observes that in that culture purses were made of ram scrotums. Thus the money used for bribing the witnesses may be in view.

27. Augustine, *Sermons to the People*, 182.

Next, we recall that Epiphany means "manifestation"; cue the "infestation" of burly dudes. And once more, intending to speak of "piqued Magi," one might conceivably picture magicians atop a mountain peak.

We could continue adducing examples, but there is no need to belabor the point given the simplicity of these strategies. But would not their simplicity seem to belie their effectiveness? How could the key to preaching by heart have been right there in children's books all along? But this may in fact be the secret of the effectiveness of the method of loci and its peculiar practices. By working with the inborn tendencies and propensities of the human mind, the Memory Palace makes learning by heart as natural as walking from your kitchen to your bedroom.

How many Pictures are needed?

Before we move on to Day 5 (Delivery), we should address a question raised by our discussion of painting potent Pictures: how many Pictures do we need? Otherwise put, how broad of a mnemonic brush should preachers paint with? In addressing this question, modern cognitive psychology provides an assist to classical rhetoric.

In an oft-cited article, "The Magical Number Seven, Plus or Minus Two," psychologist George Miller contended that our working memory—our human RAM, if you will—can only hold seven independent pieces of information at any particular time.[28] Thus, for instance, phone numbers have seven digits.[29] But there's a loophole to this, which cognitive psychologists call "chunking." "Chunking," according to Joshua Foer, "is a way to decrease the number of items you have to remember by increasing the size of each item."[30]

28. Miller, "The Magical Number Seven, Plus or Minus Two."

29. Miller offers several other examples, including the seven wonders of the world, the seven seas, the seven deadly sins, the seven notes of the musical scale, and the seven days of the week.

30. Foer, *Moonwalking with Einstein*, 61.

An example from language may suffice. Imagine you were trying to recall a string of twenty-two letters: FORGODSO-LOVEDTHEWORLD. Taken on their own this is a very difficult task; twenty-two well exceeds our mnemonic sweet spot. But when you recognize that those letters can be broken into six words— FOR GOD SO LOVED THE WORLD—suddenly, remembering them is not so hard. And if you recognize them as John 3:16, it will be easier still. Chip and Dan Heath summarize the benefits of chunking thusly: "By taking advantage of preexisting chunks of information, we can cram more information into a limited attentional space."[31] Chunking creates a kind of shortcut for the mind.

Does this have any relevance for the method of loci and the number of Pictures in the preacher's Memory Palace? Much in every way. First, chunking enables any particular Picture to "pack in" much more information than it otherwise would; images are like mnemonic power bars, containing a whole host of content. Secondly, and more pertinent at this juncture, chunking helps the preacher to break the long string of a sermon into several more memorable parts, the way we separated John 3:16 above. This happens initially in the Arrangement (*Dispositio*) stage as the message is broken up into several movements (say, seven—plus or minus two), which become the rooms of the Memory Palace.[32] And it happens again in this *Memoria* stage as the Pictures are situated throughout the Place.[33]

Using the logic of chunking, then, within each room (or movement) of the Place another set of Pictures can be included.

31. Heath and Heath, *Made to Stick*, 294.

32. For this reason it is also preferable that the chosen Place have a corresponding number of rooms. If a familiar house or building has fewer than that, that would be a reason to create the sort of hybrid real/imaginary Place as discussed in step 1 above.

33. From the perspective of cognitive psychology the argument could be made that the preacher might include up to nine Pictures in each movement (seven, plus two). Taking architecture into consideration, though, four (or less) is more optimal. This is not because four is a good round number, but because it's a good square one, so to speak: most rooms have four corners, and corners best lend themselves to the sub-movements within each room.

The result is that, rather than the sermon being limited to five to nine Pictures, it could theoretically include more than eighty.[34] More often than not, a preacher's Memory Palace will in fact have only four or five rooms, each containing about four Pictures—that is, about a quarter of what is possible. The point is that by making use of chunking the preacher is able to learn the sermon by heart much more extensively.

Day 4 (Memory) Recap

- *Memory* is the process of learning one's speech (or sermon) by heart so that it can be delivered without the use of notes
- Two steps:
  1. Pick a Place
     - Three options: Real, Imaginary, Hybrid
  2. Paint Potent Pictures
     - Technical term is *elaborative encoding*: "the formation of associative connections with other memory traces"
     - Three strategies: Association, Exaggeration, Similarity
     - Pack more content into your Pictures through "chunking"

Day 5: *Pronuntiatio* (Delivery)

At long last we come to Sunday. Time to ascend the pulpit: to "inhabit" the Memory Palace, deliver the sermon, and so invite the people of God to inhabit the word of God. In this section we will not go into detail regarding the nuances of *bonus pronuntiatio*, "good delivery"; for that, the reader is directed to the classical orators, who often discussed these nuances at length, as well as modern homiletic textbooks.[35] Rather, we will consider how one

---

34. Maxing out the limits of our working memory: nine Pictures to a room, multiplied by nine rooms. This would surely be straining the artificial memory, however, and limit how nimble the preacher can be in the sermon event itself. To switch the metaphor, it's tantamount to a computer's RAM trying to operate a dozen programs all open at once. It's possible, but decidedly suboptimal.

35. See, e.g., the *Ad Herennium* III §19–27; Quintilian's *Institutio Oratoria*

can prepare to deliver a sermon using the method of loci, and then briefly walk through the actual event of sermon delivery.

Visualizing the Memory Palace: Preparation for Delivery

Michael Phelps is standing on the edge of the pool. He is poised to dive in, preparing once again to obliterate his competition. But before he does, his longtime coach Bob Bowman gives him a command that seems utterly out of place at the pool: "Put in the videotape!" Strange as it sounds, this command to the Olympic gold medalist has relevance for preachers preparing to deliver their sermons using the method of loci.

New York Times journalist Charles Duhigg explains Bowman's "videotape" direction:

> The videotape wasn't real. Rather, it was a mental visualization of the perfect race. Each night before falling asleep and each morning after waking up, Phelps would imagine himself jumping off the blocks and, in slow motion, swimming flawlessly. He would visualize his strokes, the walls of the pool, his turns, and the finish . . . He would lie in bed with his eyes shut and watch the entire competition, the smallest details, again and again, *until he knew each second by heart.*[36]

Michael Phelps had created a mental model of his race, a 3D visual image of how it would unfold. He could then subsequently visualize himself swimming over and over again—"until he knew each second by heart."

This is something akin to how the preacher employing the method of loci prepares to deliver the sermon. Because the method relies on the symbolic and the concrete, it lends itself well to visualization. Indeed, as we noted in the Introduction, the Memory Palace may be understood as its own 3D visual image—except, of course, that it's a sermon rather than a race. Instead of imagining

---

11.3; Long, *The Witness of Preaching,* chapter 10.

36. Duhigg, *The Power of Habit,* 111 (my emphasis).

movements through the water, the preacher imagines movements through the message: introduction and conclusion, key punctuations of gospel proclamation, transitions between parts of the sermon, and so on. This accords with what Frances Yates calls a "forgotten social habit": "Who is that man moving slowly in the lonely building, stopping at intervals with an intent face? He is a rhetoric student forming a set of memory *loci*."[37] Or we might say, that's a preacher "putting in the videotape."

Preparation to preach—rehearsal, if you will—thus assumes a very different cast for the preacher using the method of loci than may often be the case for preachers. Recall from an earlier chapter that even Joseph Webb, author of *Preaching without Notes*, resorts in the last to needing dedicated time devoted to rote repetition.[38] To be sure, repetition as such is still advised; even Quintilian will counsel that "the one great art of *Memoria*" is "practice and effort."[39] But the repetition of the Memory Palace is different: less like drilling facts for a test and more like walking through plays before a game.

Due to their vivid memorability, Pictures quickly take up occupancy in the mind, and subsequently the Place may be mentally revisited many times before Sunday—even if it is just a room here and a room there. And since the Memory Palace thus fosters *visualization* (and not merely *verbalization*), such preparation is more easily done in the theater of the mind while pastors are going about their day, commuting to visits, or laying down to sleep, like Phelps imagining himself hitting the water as he hits his bed.[40] Pastors can therefore walk through their message again and again—until they are ready to preach by heart.

---

37. Yates, *The Art of Memory*, 24.

38. See Introduction; Webb, *Preaching without Notes*, 94.

39. Quintilian, *Institutio Oratoria* 11.2 §40.

40. Speaking personally, I find myself able to "walk through" a sermon a dozen times or more mentally from the time I construct my Memory Palace (usually Thursday) to the time I deliver the sermon. With each pass, the movements of the Palace become more fixed and familiar in my mind.

Leading the hearers home: Delivery Proper

Some years back I was attending a lecture by a well-known preacher. He was onstage without any notes or other props, peripatetically delivering his lecture like an Aristotelian instructor. At one point, the preacher launched into a long digression, at the conclusion of which he asked aloud, "Now, where was I?" And then, looking down at the stage and taking a few strides to his right, he said, "Ah, yes. Over here." The audience erupted in laughter.

Whether or not this preacher availed himself of the method of loci I cannot say; I only recalled this anecdote years later, after I myself had become familiar with it. His brief comment was nevertheless reflective of the experience of speaking out of the Memory Palace.[41] Let's return once more to the British mnemonist Ed Cooke for a thumbnail description of recall using the method:

> Normally memories are stored more or less at random in semantic networks, or webs of association. But you have now stored a large number of memories in a very controlled context. Because of the way spatial cognition works, all you have to do is retrace your steps through your memory palace, and hopefully at each point the images you laid down will pop back into your mind as you pass by them. All you have to do is translate those images back into the things you were trying to learn in the first place.[42]

41. It is often suggested that the locution "in the first place," etc. is a holdover from the method of loci, and one wonders whether this rhetorical question "where was I?" is not also one.

42. Quoted in Foer, *Moonwalking*, 104 (note too, apropos the previous note, Cooke's pun at the end of the quotation). Compare Matteo Ricci's advice to Governor Lu Wangai: "Once your places are all fixed in order, then you can walk through the door and make your start. Turn to the right and proceed from there. As with the practice of calligraphy, in which you move from the beginning to the end, as with fish who swim along in ordered schools, so is everything arranged in your brain, and all the images are ready for whatever you seek to remember. If you are going to use a great many [images], then let the buildings be hundreds or thousands of units in extent; if you only want a few, then take a single reception hall and just divide it up by its corners" (Ricci, "Treatise on Mnemonic Arts," 22).

Cooke is expressing the essential experience of recall by means of the method of loci. It involves two actions that happen nearly simultaneously: mental recollection and verbal expression. Mental recollection means recalling what the Pictures of the sermon signify as you retrace your steps through the Place. Verbal expression is then speaking forth the sermon from those mental prompts. As the pastor preaches, both of these steps are occurring in real time.

If this sounds overly complicated, consider an analogy: giving driving directions to your home. In your mind's eye you picture the different landmarks and turns along the way, like how Google Maps' street view can provide snapshots with its driving directions. Meanwhile, you talk to the person in need of directions: "So, you'll hang a left at Lake Street, and then come up to the post office on your right—can you picture it?" You are not necessarily explaining *what* you are picturing, but your explanation comes *by means of* what you are picturing. Retracing the familiar route is done on a kind of autopilot, freeing up the mental resources needed to articulate the directions to your conversation partner.

Something similar happens when the pastor preaches from the Memory Palace. A familiar Place functions like a well-worn path to one's workplace or favorite restaurant: you could make the trip in your sleep. The focus then becomes the Pictures along the way, which function like those landmarks when giving directions. The most challenging part, as Cooke alludes to, is the prompt retrieval of the Pictures' significance. To return to the caveat mentioned earlier in this chapter, though, when these Pictures are regarded more like mnemonics than hieroglyphs, the challenge is much less daunting; their purpose, once again, is not to conceal ideas but to encapsulate them in more "portable" form. The proclamation itself is simply a matter of speaking forth the message— of leading the hearers home. Preaching by heart from the Memory Palace thus becomes an invitation to the people of God to dwell in His word, even as the preachers themselves have manifestly made that word their home.

Day 5 (Delivery) Recap

- *Delivery* means leading your hearers to your appointed destination with words
- Visualize the Memory Palace to prepare to preach
    - Like Michael Phelps and his "videotape"
- Inhabit the Memory Palace to deliver the sermon
    - Two simultaneous actions: mental recollection and verbal expression
    - Like giving someone directions to your home: *mentally* picture your landmarks and *verbally* articulate them to your hearers

CONCLUSION
At Home in the Word

Summary of the Argument

WE HAVE NOW BROKEN down the Memory Palace piece by piece. In this concluding chapter we will put the pieces together and see the method of loci in action. First, though, we do well to review the argument thus far. For at this point, having explored in depth the full scope of the Memory Palace, the preacher might be tempted to think, "Is this really any simpler than what I'm already doing? All this talk of Places and Pictures, association and extension—it seems more complicated than it's worth." And to be sure, we have had a dizzying tour of the Memory Palace, like Chip and Joanna Gaines speeding through a "fixer-upper" on their HGTV show of that name. Take heart, preacher! For having waded through the complexities of spatial memory, elaborate encoding, and the like, we can now emerge into the liberating simplicity of the method of loci *in toto*.

To begin with, let's recall what our goal is. It is not word-for-word memorization; that is important for a stage performer or news anchor, but not necessarily for a preacher. Rather, the goal is *preaching by heart*: to internalize the essential message—the core content, the key images—of the sermon so thoroughly that the preacher can stand in the pulpit and proclaim it without notes as a Spirit-prompted utterance. In so doing, a greater degree of harmony may be achieved between the preacher's deliberations and delivery, preparations and proclamation, and thus the credibility of the message (and the messenger) is increased.

In order to reach this goal we enlisted the help of classical rhetoric. In Part I we reviewed some elements of Greek and Roman oratory that are not only relevant to the contemporary preaching task generally, but are even more so—closer to our present concerns—helpful for preaching by heart: Aristotle's modes of persuasion (noting especially the relationship of memorization and *ethos*) and the so-called "canons" of rhetoric, of which *Memoria* ("memory") is part. We then narrowed our focus to *Memoria* and the method of loci. In that section we heard from several of the ancient masters—Cicero and Quintilian, among others—in order to fill out a picture of this classical practice also known as the Memory Palace.

In Part II we applied the lessons of classical rhetoric and the method of loci to the preacher's task today. We saw how, with an eye toward preaching by heart, the canons of rhetoric provide a framework for preparing to preach that privileges the actual *delivery* of the sermon, rather than just its *composition*. Then we delved into the nitty-gritty of "constructing" a Memory Palace and observed its value for preaching. First, a well-chosen Place leverages the spatial memory, enabling preachers to "walk through" the corridors of the mind as naturally as walking through the rooms of their homes. Then, as their sermonic content is painted into potent Pictures—vivid images that point up the essential details—the message becomes both more refined (like those Homeric epics that left behind needless abstractions) and more memorable. And finally, using the logic of "chunking," more material than one might have thought possible is "packed into" the preacher's set of Pictures. Put together, with the Memory Palace preachers have something like a three-dimensional, virtual reality outline that they can experience and employ in real time.

Preaching by Heart—Step by Step

Day 1: *Inventio* (Discovery)

☐   Gather the raw material of the sermon through study of Scripture and secondary sources

☐   Generate a focus or theme

Day 2: *Dispositio* (Arrangement)

☐   Complete the one-sentence sermon exercise

☐   Determine what Structure best suits the message

Day 3: *Elocutio* (Style)

☐   Sketch the sermon

☐   Focus on the concrete elements of story and metaphor

Day 4: *Memoria* (Memory)

☐   Pick a Place (Real/Imaginary/Hybrid)

☐   Paint potent Pictures (Association/Exaggeration/Similarity)

Day 5: *Pronuntiatio* (Delivery)

☐   Visualize the sermon

☐   Lead the hearers home

Putting the pieces together

Thus our argument has unfolded. And now, it's time to put the pieces together and see the method of loci in action. We got a taste of this in the last chapter as we worked backwards—reverse-engineering, so to speak, some selections from St. Augustine. This is useful as an analytical exercise to understand parts of the art of memory, but in order to grasp the actual practice of preparing to preach by means of the Memory Palace it will be more helpful to walk sequentially through the method's steps. And so in this concluding chapter I am going to take you through the process as I used it for a sermon that I myself preached. To do this, we will travel once again through the days of preparation and their corresponding canons. My hope is that as we "put in the videotape" like Michael Phelps and envision this sermon unfolding, you will become more confident to use the Memory Palace for yourself.

Day 1: Inventio (Discovery)

Our text is from John 14, especially verses 1–3: "[Jesus said:] Let not your hearts be troubled. Believe in God; believe also in me. In my Father's house are many rooms. If it were not so, would I have told you that I go to prepare a place for you? And if I go and prepare a place for you, I will come again and will take you to myself, that where I am you may be also."[1] As a preacher, this text is a softball. Its familiar cadences, evocative images, and consoling message make it a joy to preach. That being said, the challenge for a text such as this can be in narrowing what to focus on; in addition to the rich theology in those first few verses quoted, you also have Jesus' famous lines in verse 6: "I am the way, and the truth, and the life. No one comes to the Father except through me." And so this could be an opportunity to preach on the "scandal of particularity," the hope of heaven, or peace in the midst of uncertainty—to name only a few themes. After devoting a good deal of time to study of the text (as set out in chapter 3 above), I settle on my theme: the church triumphant, the Christian teaching about the saints in heaven—or, as Jesus puts it, "in the Father's house." With this focus in view, I am ready to determine a structure for the message.

Day 2: Dispositio (Arrangement)

A theme such as the church triumphant lends itself well to several structures. For instance, a natural option would be a compare/contrast structure in which the "church militant" (i.e., the saints living on earth) is set alongside the "church triumphant" (i.e., the saints living in heaven). Another possibility would be to consider some of the ramifications of this doctrine for Christian living according

---

1. John 14:1–14 is the appointed Gospel reading for the fifth Sunday of Easter (Series A) in the Revised Common Lectionary.

to a cause-and-effect structure: belief in the church triumphant (the cause) leads to hopeful grieving, grateful praying, and joyful receiving of Holy Communion (the effects). After concluding my One Sentence Sermon exercise, though (outlined in chapter 3), I decided to go with the Four Pages structure popularized by Paul Scott Wilson.[2] In Wilson's design, the sermon is structured around four movements: (1) trouble in the text, (2) trouble in the world, (3) grace in the text, and (4) grace in the world. Adding an introduction, I now have a five-part structure for my sermon. This will be important when it comes to selecting the Place and plotting the sermon as part of my Memory Palace.

Day 3: Elocutio (Style)

The main task of my Style day, as discussed in the section in chapter 3, is to sketch out the core content of the sermon, focusing especially on the concrete language that I will use to convey it. At this point I am not attempting to fill in every last detail of the message, but to establish three or four points that I wish to make in each of the sermon's five movements. And in passing I note here another way in which the process of the Memory Palace impinges upon my preparations for preaching: knowing that in each movement I will only want to develop a handful of Pictures ("seven, plus or minus two"[3]), I sketch accordingly.

Rather than pretend that I am more organized or thorough than I actually am, I am going to share with you the controlled chaos that is the sketch of my *Elocutio* work (see Figure 3 below). You'll notice two things here. First, the form appears much like any other outline (though I am not picky about following the proper hierarchy of Roman numerals, capital letters, etc.). This is by design: again, the end product of the Memory Palace is something like a 3D outline in my mind, and consequently I find it most helpful for the precursor already to take that form. Second, the content

2. Wilson, *The Four Pages of the Sermon.*

3. See above on chunking in chapter 4.

is more abbreviated and impressionistic than what you might typically find in an outline. My goal is not to write an abridged form of the sermon, but to distill the essential content for each movement. Some will prefer to sketch out a more extensive outline at this point, or even a manuscript; this is fine, so long as you remember this is still part of the process for *preparing to preach* and not the sermon itself. By not overcomplicating your sketch on Day 3, you make your life easier on Day 4 when you construct your Memory Palace. To that we now turn.

Figure 3: Sermon sketch

I. Introduction
1) Muppets Xmas: "Life is made up of meetings and partings; that is the way of it"—but must it always be so?...
2) Easter in Exile: the Church is still the Church "within the Father's house"...
3) Church in three modes: Militant, Glorified, and what we're discussing today—Triumphant...
4) This teaching brings balm to the soul smarting from partings—where we find the disciples...

II. Trouble in the text
1) Jesus' first word in today's Gospel: "Let not your hearts be troubled"—Why?...
2) Judas' betrayal, Peter's denial, and—most of all—Jesus' parting: "Where I'm going you cannot come"...
3) Shattering news: they've left everything—abandoned boats, burned bridges—and now He's going to *leave* them?!...
4) Their hearts are roiled like stormy waters, b/c being separated from the One you love is sharpest pain of all...

III. Trouble in the world
1) Brought home to me in a dumb-parent move: last spring, returning from a shopping trip—where's Ellie?...
2) She's weeping and gnashing her teeth, out in the car for nearly an hour...
3) Theological application: Hell = separation from God...
4) Personal application: you know this pain of being parted from a loved one...

IV. Grace in the text
1) Jesus' proclamation: "In my Father's house..."—a circumlocution for saying "heaven," but why not just say "in heaven there's many dwelling places"?...
2) Point isn't *place* (which can become a distraction), but *personal presence*...
3) Jesus' goal = where He is, we'd be...
4) To that end: Romans 14.8-9 → He was separated that nothing would separates us...

V. Grace in the world
1) This is the significance of the Church Triumphant: nothing separates us from Christ *or* His Body...
2) Jesus = I AM (way, truth, life)—follow Him in the way that leads to the Father's house...
3) Communion of saints—"Oh, blest communion": the crazy glue of baptismal water and the Body & Blood of Christ...
4) The Church entire awaits that "yet more glorious day" when Jesus will come again—partings no more. Amen.

Day 4: Memoria (Memory)

Now we have come to the Memory Palace proper. Recall the two steps to this stage that we set out in chapter 4: 1) Pick a Place (*locus*); and 2) Paint potent Pictures (*imagines*). Let's walk through both of these steps, seeing how our Memory Palace takes shape.

Step 1: Pick a Place

To reiterate our previous advice, the most important criterion for picking your Place is familiarity. You do not want to be thinking about the movements that are necessary from room to room, or how you get from the foyer to the kitchen. Rather, the Place should be so ingrained in your memory that you could sleepwalk through it; indeed, a good rule of thumb might be that if you have *actually* sleepwalked through a place it will make for a good Memory Palace *locus*.

For me, this is a simple step. For most of my sermons I simply use my home, which in addition to being a very familiar place has the added benefit of being a Colonial style house that lends itself well to diagramming: the first floor has a central foyer, with rooms encircling the staircase. Depending on the sermon structure, and thus the number of movements that are entailed, I can even leave out or include some rooms (e.g. my study, which is attached on the back of the house). You can picture a simplified diagram of the Place in Figure 4.

Figure 4: The Place

| III. Study— Trouble in the world | | IV. Kitchen— Grace in the text |
| II. Living room— Trouble in the text | I. Foyer— Introduction | V. Dining room— Grace in the world |

Step 2: Paint Potent Pictures

Now things get really fun. Remember that the goal at this stage is to associate the content from the sermon sketch with unforgettable images that will prompt recall of the message. This step is the heart of the method of loci. Keep in mind here the different strategies for painting Pictures that we discussed in chapter 4: Association, Exaggeration, and Similarity. As I lay this out, you will see them all operative. You will also want to keep a finger on the sketch in Figure 1 above, so that you can discern how the Pictures correspond to the content of the sermon.[4]

4. Fair warning: as I take you through the Pictures for my own Memory Palace for this sermon, you'll get a glimpse into the strange world of my mind's machinations. You've been advised.

Introduction: In the Introduction, I start with a quote from Bob Cratchit ("played" by Kermit the Frog) in *The Muppet Christmas Carol*, but then call the sentiment of the quote into question. And so here I'll have Kermit furiously shaking his fist in a rage, as if to say "it can't be so!" at my venerable teacher, Will Willimon, of *Resident Aliens* fame. He turns up as a Picture because the next move I want to make is to give a recap of the sermon series, entitled "Easter in Exile" (hence *Resident Aliens*). The enraged Kermit berates the surprised Willimon, the both of whom are suddenly attacked by Triumph the Insult Comic Dog[5]—a natural Picture for me to introduce the theme of "church *triumphant*." This movement is rounded out by Triumph apologizing for his outburst by applying balm to the smarting Kermit and Willimon, recalling the benefit of this teaching of the Church Triumphant for the hearers.[6]

Are you getting a feel for the delightful—and memorable— weirdness of the Memory Palace?

Second Movement: Now we move into the living room and the second movement of the sermon: Trouble in the Text. The first thing we find is a bunch of harried, hopping hearts—blood-pumping, arteries bulging, *hearts*. Gross. These hearts are "troubled," no question; these are just what Jesus comes to quell. Before you can linger too long on that, though, there's a commotion as my brother, Peter, bolts from Jeff Tweedy, lead singer of Wilco. Tweedy, who once crooned (echoing the words of Jesus), "Where I am going you cannot come," is hurling a rooster at poor Pete, a Picture that for me evokes the reasons those hearts are hopping: Peter's betrayal, Jesus' departure. Poor Peter flees Tweedy only to run headlong into Gallagher—yes, *that* Gallagher—who is shattering not watermelons but boats and bridges, like an apostle who has left everything. This supremely unsettling scene crescendos with Michael Stipe, riding a surfboard atop roiling waters, and longingly singing that

---

5. Triumph was a puppet and regular character on Conan O'Brien, which enjoyed insulting the celebrity guests on the show. I told you I was giving fair warning.

6. See a visual depiction of this in Figure 3.

"this one goes out to the one I love . . ." The pain of parting smarts like none other.[7]

Third Movement: The third movement of the sermon is back in the study, where there is Trouble in the World (ain't that the truth). Straightaway, you come across Lloyd Christmas of *Dumb and Dumber* carrying a sack of groceries, which recalls for me the dumb dad move I made last year after a trip to the supermarket. Illustrating this pain of parting, the story goes that I forgot to bring in my two-year-old daughter, Ellie, from the car. So there's Ellie in my Memory Palace, weeping and gnashing her teeth—just like how I found her on that unfortunate afternoon (not to worry, she was otherwise fine and has since forgiven me). Turning from Ellie, I find Sandra Bullock as an astronaut in *Gravity*, suffocating for lack of oxygen—a Picture I create to recall how hell, the ultimate separation, is like suffocation of the soul. In her thrashing, Sandra smacks none other than the bard himself, William Shakespeare, who once wrote that "parting is such sweet sorrow." For most of us, though, that's a hard pill to swallow.

Fourth Movement: We have now made it to the kitchen, and while there's now Grace in the Text, there's no respite in this fourth movement of the Memory Palace. You hear the thumping beats of the '90s Christian rock band, Audio Adrenaline? They're rocking out to their hit "Big House" (based on John 14), when suddenly my friend and mentor, David Schmitt—who provided for me the insight that Jesus speaks of the many rooms of his Father's house to underscore that the point isn't so much the *place* as it is the *personal presence* of God—leaps over the band and dunks on Colton Burpo, the famous little boy from *Heaven Is for Real.* David comes back down only to be ambushed by an army of My Buddies, a terrifying toy from my youth that had the obnoxious ear worm of a jingle, "My buddy, my buddy, wherever I go *he-e-e goes.*"[8] Fortunately, the army of My Buddies is brushed aside by an army of

7. See Figure 4 for a visual depiction.

8. I apologize for putting that song into your head. This is one of the downsides of the Memory Palace, as you often find yourself exploiting this sort of awfully unforgettable ephemera.

fourteen Romans, who promptly fall into the abyss of a crevasse that has opened in the corner of the kitchen (not sure if insurance will cover that). This strange Picture brings to mind how I plan to preach how Jesus was separated from the Father and went down into the abyss of death for us.

Fifth Movement: Finally, we come to the Dining Room and to Grace in the World. Here we're reunited with Triumph the Insult Comic Dog, who is now inexplicably clinging to a crucifix, inseparable from the Savior. Triumph then becomes distracted by hip-hop icon Eminem (who had a hit song with the recurring refrain, "I AM . . ."), skipping merrily along with theologian David Bentley Hart, who more than any other has taught me the significance of God being the One in whom we "live and move and have our being." From there I hear a struggle in the corner: a pious couple from my parish, who grasp the profound significance of the communion of saints, has evidently crazy-glued themselves to the baptismal font! But not to worry, that great advocate of the resurrection and new creation, N. T. Wright, liberates them from their bondage and then chastises Kermit/Cratchit (who has made another appearance) for being resigned to persistent partings.

Amen.

The ridiculousness of this scene is not lost on me. To the contrary, as we have taken pains to demonstrate, it is that very ridiculousness that is the "special sauce" of the Memory Palace. Outrageous images peppered throughout a well-known location: that's the essence of the method of loci. Lest the reader be put off by the complexity of this discursive account, notice how—shorn of the narrative flourishes—it is deceptively straightforward. You have:

1) A cast of characters (Triumph, Gallagher, et al.)

2) with unlikely props (hopping hearts, crazy glue, etc.)

3) engaged in surprising activities (dunking, falling into crevasses, etc.)

4) in a familiar location (my house).

And let the reader also understand that for to me to narrate this discursively—entertaining as it may be—is far more toil than to conjure up the scenes in my mind's eye. The purpose of these dynamic Pictures is merely to serve as prompts for the already-prepared content of the sermon—and note well, it is unquestionably easier to recall one's own Pictures and their significances rather than those of someone else (such as this author). Thus, the essentials of the method are uncomplicated, even if their embellishments might give the impression that it's otherwise. In the end, it's simply a system of Places and Pictures, employed for the goal of preaching by heart.

Day 5: Pronuntiatio (Delivery)

The actual Delivery of this sermon is available on YouTube should the reader wish to view it.[9] Let me share a couple of brief words of reflection on my final preparations for Delivery and the Delivery itself. When it comes to the visualization ("putting in the video-tape"), I find that two practices are especially helpful. First, I have created a simple diagram that imitates my Place, on which I write the Picture ideas in with my chicken scratch (see Figure 5 below). Second, I will actually walk through my house—which, recall, is the *locus* that I use—visualizing the different movements of the sermon as I go. Indeed, in my experience this simple habit alone improves recall enormously.

9. I am writing this amid the COVID-19 quarantine of 2020, and the sermon was preached as part of my congregation's online stream. It may be viewed at https://youtu.be/LYojNf8mYTo?t=928.

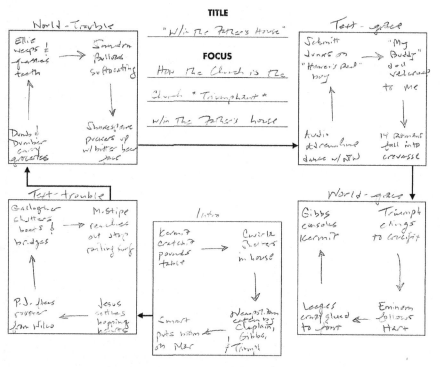

In terms of the Delivery itself, as with most Sundays by the time I got to this point I was able to give myself fully to the proclamation of the Word. Occasionally I will digress a little bit, but asking "where was I?" I am able quickly to regain my place. As we have stressed throughout this book, it will take practice and effort to master the skill of preaching with the method of loci. Before too long, though, just like when learning the route to a new destination, it will become second nature for preachers. Yes, they will know the way by heart.

Why I am not persuasive

In a provocative short essay for *Homiletic* entitled "Why I Am Not Persuasive," Richard Lischer asks a question that raises an important issue for us in concluding this study.[10] "Why would anyone wish *not* to be persuasive," asks Lischer, "especially a preacher, of all people, whose success depends on his or her ability to win an audience?" He goes on to invoke the parable of the Sower—in particular the pure prodigality of the Sower, casting the seed of the word hither and yon without discretion. Little about the parable suggests that any potency belongs to the preacher. Thus, Lischer writes, "To insist on 'persuasion' as a paradigm for the sowing and germination of the word of God simply does not do justice to the environment in which we live and minister."[11] This is a necessary qualification for any discussion of rhetoric in preaching, such as this book has advanced.

But Lischer makes an additional point that is closer to the heart of the concerns that animated this book, and takes us back to where we started. He writes,

> It occurred to me that over the years I have not seen any preacher improve dramatically by focusing on persuasion either as a technique or a goal. I have seen no preachers change—really change—by working on their imagery or seeking the perfect glass slipper of form. The transformations I have witnessed occurred in those who caught fire in other ways, who, for example, surrendered themselves to the Holy Spirit, or renewed their devotion to Christ, or gave themselves to some practice of ministry only to be surprised by renewal . . . Mysteriously, they all became changed preachers![12]

The Memory Palace is a technique, a tool, and the foregoing argument of this book has sought to establish its value for preachers. But Lischer's comments return us to an assertion and assumption stated in the Introduction: that preachers actually *believe* what they preach—that their own hearts are so gripped by the good news that they desire to speak it forth in a way that does justice to its truth not only in their lives, but in the world.

10. Lischer, "Why I Am Not Persuasive."
11. Lischer, "Why I Am Not Persuasive," 14.
12. Lischer, "Why I Am Not Persuasive," 15–16.

If the preacher does not share that core conviction, no amount of classical rhetoric or clever mnemonics will help him to preach by heart. But if, on the other hand, the preacher does in fact make his home in the Word of God, inhabits the good news of Christ risen to renovate the hearts of humanity through the power of the Spirit and the proclamation of the gospel, and therefore desires to preach by heart more faithfully, thus leading the people of God similarly to be at home in that word, then this preacher knows of no better method to reach that goal than the Memory Palace. My hope is that the reader is likewise persuaded.

BIBLIOGRAPHY

Aristotle. *Ars Rhetorica.* Translated by J. H. Freese. Revised by Gisela Striker. Loeb Classical Library 193. Cambridge, MA: Harvard University Press, 2020.

———. *De Anima. Parva Naturalia. On Breath.* Translated by W. S. Hett. Loeb Classical Library 288. Cambridge, MA: Harvard University Press, 1975.

Arthurs, Jeffrey. *Preaching with Variety.* Grand Rapids: Kregel, 2007.

Augustine of Hippo. *Confessions.* Translated by Henry Chadwick. Oxford: Oxford University Press, 1991.

———. *On Christian Teaching.* Oxford: Oxford University Press, 1999.

———. *Sermons to the People.* Translated by William Griffin. New York: Image, 2002.

Bacon, Francis. *De Augmentis.* New York: Cambridge University Press, 2011.

Broadus, John A. *A Treatise on the Preparation and Delivery of Sermons.* New York: A. C. Armstrong and Son, 1899.

Brown, Scott C., and Fergus I. M. Craik. "Encoding and Retrieval of Information." In *The Oxford Handbook of Memory,* edited by Endel Tulving, 93–107. Oxford: Oxford University Press, 2000.

Buttrick, David. *Homiletic Moves and Structures.* Minneapolis: Fortress, 1987.

Church, F. F. "Rhetorical Structure and Design in Paul's Letter to Philemon." *Harvard Theological Review* 71.1–2 (1978) 17–33.

Cicero. *De Inventione. The Best Kind of Orator. Topics.* Translated by H. M. Hubbell. Loeb Classical Library 386. Cambridge, MA: Harvard University Press, 1949.

———. *De Oratore. Books 1–2.* Translated by E. W. Sutton and H. Rackham. Loeb Classical Library 348. Cambridge, MA: Harvard University Press, 1942.

———. *Brutus. Orator.* Translated by G. L. Hendrickson and H. M. Hubbell. Loeb Classical Library 342. Cambridge, MA: Harvard University Press, 1939.

CNN.com. "Winfrey stands behind 'Pieces' author." January 12, 2006. http://www.cnn.com/2006/SHOWBIZ/books/01/11/frey.lkl/index.html.

Cohen, Steve. *Win the Crowd*. New York: HarperCollins, 2005.

Corbett, Edward. *Classical Rhetoric for the Modern Student*. Oxford: Oxford University Press, 1998

Covey, Steven. *First Things First*. New York: Fireside, 1994.

Deferrari, Roy J. "St. Augustine's Method of Composing and Delivering Sermons." *The American Journal of Philology* 43.3 (1922) 193–219.

Duhigg, Charles. *The Power of Habit*. New York: Random House, 2012.

Dunn-Wilson, David. *A Mirror for the Church: Preaching in the First Five Centuries*. Grand Rapids: Eerdmans, 2005.

Edwards, O. C., Jr. *A History of Preaching*. Nashville: Abingdon, 2004.

Fant, Clyde. "Memory." In *The Concise Encyclopedia of Preaching*, edited by William Willimon and Richard Lischer, 330–32. Louisville: Westminster John Knox, 1995.

Foer, Joshua. *Moonwalking With Einstein*. New York: Penguin, 2011.

Frakt, Austin. "An Ancient and Proven Way to Improve Memorization; Go Ahead and Try It." *The New York Times*, March 24, 2016. https://www. nytimes.com/2016/03/24/upshot/an-ancient-and-proven-way-to-improve-memory-go-ahead-and-try-it.html.

Gallo, Carmine. *Talk Like TED*. New York: St. Martin's, 2014.

Graves, Michael P. "Ministry and Preaching." In *The Oxford Handbook of Quaker Studies*, edited by Stephen Angell, 277–91. Oxford: Oxford University Press, 2013.

Groome, David. *An Introduction to Cognitive Psychology*. 3rd ed. New York: Psychology, 2014.

Haidt, Jonathan. *The Righteous Mind*. New York: Parthenon, 2012.

Havelock, Eric. *Preface to Plato*. Cambridge, MA: Harvard University Press, 1963.

Heath, Chip, and Dan Heath. *Made to Stick*. New York: Random House, 2007.

Houser, William. "Puritan Homiletics: A Caveat." *Concordia Theological Quarterly* 53.4 (1989) 255–70.

Jensen, Richard. *Thinking in Story: Preaching in a Post-Literate Age*. Lima, OH: CSS, 1993.

Justin Martyr. *Second Apology*. https://ccel.org/ccel/justin_martyr/second_apology/anfo1.

Kennedy, George. *Classical Rhetoric and Its Christian and Secular Tradition from Ancient to Modern Times*. Chapel Hill, NC: University of North Carolina Press, 1999.

———. *The New Testament and Rhetorical Criticism*. Chapel Hill, NC: University of North Carolina Press, 1984.

Koller, Charles. *How to Preach without Notes*. Grand Rapids: Baker Academic, 2011.

Legge, Eric, Christopher R. Madan, Enoch T. Ng, and Jeremy B. Caplan. "Building a memory palace in minutes: Equivalent memory performance using virtual versus conventional environments with the Method of Loci." *Acta psychologica* 141.3 (2012) 380–90.

Lischer, Richard. "Why I Am Not Persuasive." *Homiletic* 26 (1999) 13–16.

Long, Thomas. *The Witness of Preaching.* 3rd ed. Louisville: Westminster John Knox, 2016.

Longinus. *On the Sublime.* In Aristotle, Longinus, Demetrius, *Poetics, On the Sublime, On Style.* Translated by Stephen Halliwell, W. Hamilton Fyfe, Doreen C. Innes, and W. Rhys Roberts. Revised by Donald A. Russell. Loeb Classical Library 199. Cambridge, MA: Harvard University Press, 1995.

Lowry, Eugene. *The Homiletical Plot.* Louisville: Westminster John Knox, 2001.

McPhee, John. "Structure." *The New Yorker,* January 14, 2013, 46–55.

Miller, George. "The Magical Number Seven, Plus or Minus Two: Some Limits on Our Capacity for Processing Information." *Psychological Review* 63 (1956) 81–97.

O'Keefe, John J., and Russell R. Reno. *Sanctified Vision: An Introduction to Early Christian Interpretation of the Bible.* Baltimore: Johns Hopkins University Press, 2005.

Old, Hugh Oliphant. *The Reading and Preaching of the Scriptures in the Worship of the Christian Church.* Grand Rapids: Eerdmans, 1998.

Ong, Walter. *Orality and Literacy.* New York: Methuen, 1982.

Overdorf, Daniel. *One Year to Better Preaching.* Grand Rapids: Kregel, 2013.

Parish, Peggy. *Play Ball, Amelia Bedelia.* New York: Harper & Row, 1972.

Pattison, T. Harwood. *The Making of the Sermon.* Philadelphia: American Baptist Publication Society, 1902.

Pinker, Steven. *The Sense of Style.* New York: Viking, 2014.

Plato. *Euthyphro. Apology. Crito. Phaedo. Phaedrus.* Translated by Harold North Fowler. Loeb Classical Library 36. Cambridge, MA: Harvard University Press, 1914.

Plutarch. *Life of Demosthenes. Lives, Volume VII: Demosthenes and Cicero. Alexander and Caesar.* Translated by Bernadotte Perrin. Loeb Classical Library 99. Cambridge, MA: Harvard University Press, 1919.

Postman, Neil. *Amusing Ourselves to Death.* New York: Penguin, 1986.

Pseudo-Cicero. *Rhetorica ad Herennium.* Loeb Classical Library 403. Translated by Harry Caplan. Cambridge, MA: Harvard University Press, 1954.

Quintilian. *Institutio Oratoria.* Edited and translated by Donald A. Russell. Loeb Classical Library 124–27, 494. Cambridge, MA: Harvard University Press, 2002.

Ricci, Matteo. "Treatise on Mnemonic Arts." In *Source Materials on Christianity in Asia,* edited by Wu Xiangxiang, 22. Taipei: 1964.

Robinson, Haddon. *Biblical Preaching.* 2d ed. Grand Rapids: Baker, 2001.

Salinger, J. D. *Franny and Zooey.* New York: Bantam, 1961.

Schmitt, David R. "Richard Caemmerer's Goal, Malady, Means: A Retrospective Glance." *Concordia Theological Quarterly* 74 (2010) 23–38.

———. "Sermon Structures." https://concordiatheology.org/sermon-structs/.

Seuss, Dr. *And to Think that I Saw it on Mulberry Street.* New York: Random House, 1937.

Small, Brian C. "The Use of Rhetorical *Topoi* in the Characterization of Jesus in the Book of Hebrews." *Perspectives in Religious Studies* 37 (2010) 53–69.

Spence, Jonathan. *The Memory Palace of Matteo Ricci*. New York: Penguin, 1983.

Stanley, Andy. *Communicating for a Change*. Colorado Springs, CO: Multnomah, 2006.

Strunk, William, and E. B. White. *The Elements of Style*. 4th ed. New York: Longman, 1999.

Sunukjian, Donald. *Invitation to Biblical Preaching*. Grand Rapids: Kregel, 2007.

Sweet, Leonard. *Post-Modern Pilgrims*. Nashville: Broadman & Holman, 2000.

Van Edwards, Vanessa. "5 Secrets of a Successful TED Talk." *The Huffington Post*. https://www.huffingtonpost.com/vanessa-van-edwards/5-secrets-of-a-successful_b_6887472.html.

Voelz, James W. *What Does This Mean?* St. Louis: CPH, 1997.

Ware, Henry, Jr. *Hints on Extemporaneous Preaching*. Boston: Cummings, Hilliard, & Co., 1824.

Webb, Joseph. *Preaching without Notes*. Nashville: Abingdon, 2001.

Wilson, Paul Scott. *The Practice of Preaching*. 2d ed. Nashville: Abingdon, 2007.

———. *The Four Pages of the Sermon*. Nashville: Abingdon, 2010.

Yates, Frances. *The Art of Memory*. New York: Routledge, 1966.

Zielinski, Sarah. "The Secret of Sherlock's Mind Palace." Smithsonian.com. https://www.smithsonianmag.com/arts-culture/secrets-sherlocks-mind-palace-180949567/.

Printed in Great Britain
by Amazon

25147416R00078